CONTENTS

How To
IMPROVE YOUR MEMORY AND CONCENTRATION

PROPERTY OF
U.S. ARMY

by **MICHAEL C. KELLETT**

MONARCH
PRESS

Dedication
To my darling Marlene

First Printing: 1983
Copyright © 1977 by
Michael C. Kellett

Published by
MONARCH PRESS
A Division of Simon & Schuster, Inc.
Simon & Schuster Building
1230 Avenue of the Americas
New York, N.Y. 10020

MONARCH PRESS and colophon are registered trademarks
of Simon & Schuster, Inc.

10 9 8 7 6 5 4 3 2 1

ISBN: 0-671-49237-3

Printed in the United States of America

INTRODUCTION

Memory is the ability to re-create and recall something that we experienced, or saw, or knew, or read. Some people tend to identify memory with extrasensory perception, clairvoyance, mental telepathy, and other psychic phenomena. There is no connection between memory and these as yet unproven phenomena, and there is nothing "psychic" or mysterious about memory. People who have excellent memories possess no special mental powers. They have good memories because, consciously or not, they are applying the right techniques in the right situations.

Can memory be improved? The answer is yes. We often hear people say, "I have a poor memory," or "I have a good memory for numbers but a poor one for names." Such statements reveal their mistaken belief that memory is something over which we have no control. It is true that a certain amount of inherent intelligence is necessary in remembering, and that there are physical differences that may affect memory. What is important to bear in mind, however, is that memory is a faculty that can be developed and improved regardless of inherent differences.

What is concentration? Stated simply, concentration is the ability to keep our mind on whatever it is we are doing, or thinking, or reading, or seeing. In other words, it's our ability to "stay on the track." How many times have you read an article, listened to a lecture or been simply conversing when you suddenly realized that your mind was wandering? This book will help you to recognize some causes of mind-wandering and show you how to cut down on this serious time-wasting tendency.

Can the ability to concentrate be developed? Of course it can. With all the distractions among which we live, it is not surprising that our minds often "stray." We can

1

learn how to modify this tendency. It may not be easy to do, but neither is it too difficult.

Here are some areas in which improving your memory and your ability to concentrate can help you:

1. *Communication.* Have you ever felt certain, after you have read an article or listened to a lecture, that you understood it all and were certain to remember what you understood?

    Well, such certainty would serve you well if you were to take a multiple-choice or true-false test. But suppose you were not taking such a test and had to write an essay, or were asked to say what the article or lecture was about. Improving your *mental organization* and your ability to concentrate can help you to recall on such occasions, and also to improve your reading speed, your writing and speaking ability, and even your thinking.

2. *Recall.* Suppose you are having dinner with friends and would like to tell a joke or relate an anecdote that is exactly in line with the conversation. You've told many jokes and related many anecdotes before, and yet, somehow, on this occasion you can't think of a single one to tell. Then, when the party is over, and you are driving home, you find, to your dismay, that you can think of a number of "good ones." Here, too, you can prevent such a situation by applying the techniques of memory discussed in this book. They will enable you to remember what you wish and when you wish — and not later.

3. *Specific areas of memory.* Using the techniques of memory makes it possible for you to apply them to such specific areas as remembering numbers, names, faces, tasks, chores, and places — with surprising facility.

4. *Human understanding.* Last but not least, there is the need to learn more about yourself and others. This book will give you an insight into how the

human mind works with regard to memory and how psychology can be applied in everyday life. You will recognize that where memory is concerned, all human beings are subject to a fairly consistent set of psychological principles and that we always remember or forget for a reason. A knowledge of why people forget, and the kind of situations and conditions that are likely to cause forgetting, can not only be helpful in developing your own memory, but will also enable you to help others to remember your words and ideas.

It is not enough to just read and understand the contents of this book. You must implement your reading and understanding by thinking, reacting, and *doing*. You must be alert to opportunities that will enable you to apply the principles and techniques offered. If, for example, you are learning to read in a certain way that will enable you to remember what you have read, you must continue to read in that way. Once you have fixed the ideas and principles offered in this book in your mind, you must keep on using them in every way possible. Improving your memory and developing your ability to concentrate are *skills* and you can acquire them with this book and with continuing practice.

Chapter One

WHAT MAKES US FORGET?

Everybody forgets and everybody remembers. If we did not forget our minds would be overburdened; if we did not remember, our minds would be empty. Forgetting cannot be avoided. It allows us to stop remembering what is no longer useful and thus enables us to absorb new information.

The problem in forgetting is not that we forget per se but that we forget some things that we have consciously tried to remember. The mechanism of memory works independently of conscious thought.

The conscious mind certainly affects memory by its power to direct attention, but *it does not control memory*. We cannot consciously decide what or for how long we want to remember. Simply saying to yourself after reading a chapter in a textbook "I must remember what I have just read" is not a guarantee that you will remember it.

If our memory were subject to our conscious direction, we would have to keep on interrupting our thoughts and actions to direct what we wish to remember and what we wish to forget. Through the process of forgetting, our brain has a way of deciding this for us, without the aid of conscious thought. Let us be thankful that our memory system is just the way it is. Let us regard it as a systematic organization, subject to general but consistent guidelines. This can help us to understand why even the things we regard as important are forgotten.

The Basic Reason for Forgetting

Interference is the basic reason for forgetting. It is commonly believed that the passage of time explains for-

4

getting. While this cannot be entirely refuted, there is more to forgetting than the passage of time. Let's set up a series of imaginary situations. Our object will be to see which conditions or situations will result in the most forgetting.

Suppose we memorize a list of shopping items. Between the time we memorize them and the time we need to remember them, we will, of course, have engaged in some other activity. What if our intervening activity were sleep? How much memory loss or forgetting would occur in sleep as compared with a waking activity? Surprisingly, very little. It is during normal wakefulness that most forgetting occurs. When we are awake we engage in mental and physical activities. These activities cause *interference*, and it is interference that is the underlying cause of forgetting.

The most common form of interference occurs when thought or learning processes take place between the time when something is learned and when it has to be recalled. This is called *retroactive interference*. We learn "A," then we learn or think about "B," and then we are asked to recall "A." *Pro-active interference* occurs when something learned inhibits future learning, for example, when a secretary who has learned to type on one kind of typewriter finds it difficult to type on another kind.

Intensity of Interference

We will examine the concept of interference a little more closely. Using the shopping list as an example once again, let's compare the interfering effects of two mental activities. Suppose an easy ride in a car is the intervening activity between learning and recall. How would that compare with a ride through heavy traffic? Certainly, the amount of time spent in heavy traffic would cause more forgetting, more interference, than the same amount of time spent in a relaxing drive. We can now arrive at the principle that forgetting depends, to a large extent, on the *intensity* of the intervening activity and the *degree of tension* experienced.

The Degree of Similarity

The following hypothetical situations are a bit more difficult. (1) Which intervening activity would cause more interference between the time we learn a shopping list and the time we need to recall it: doing math problems or learning another shopping list? All other factors being equal, learning another shopping list would cause more forgetting. (2) What mental activity would cause more forgetting immediately following the learning of a telephone number? The answer: learning another telephone number. And another principle emerges: Retention loss varies, depending on the degree of similarity between the original and the interjected activity.

Many experiments have shown how different activities affect interference. In one study, university students were given a list of adjectives to memorize. Between the learning sessions and recall of the adjectives, an activity was interjected. It was found that the number of adjectives recalled varied according to nature of the interjected activity:

Interpolated Activity	Adjectives Recalled
reading jokes	45
learning 3-place numbers	37
learning nonsense syllables	26
learning adjectives unrelated to originals	22
learning antonyms of originals	18
learning synonyms of originals	12

It can readily be seen that the more the interpolated material is like the original, the greater the interference.

Implications of the Interference Theory

It would seem that how long and how well something is remembered depends to a large extent on the nature of the intervening activity. Keeping this in mind can help us to ascertain with greater accuracy whether or not something will be remembered, and how long it will take to remember it.

We all have a tendency to overestimate our ability to remember. Often we are so sure of ourselves that we fail to write down, or review, or take special steps to recall — and sure enough, we forget. Sometimes we berate ourselves for forgetting when we really presented our memory system with an almost impossible task.

The wife who asks her husband at breakfast to stop by the cleaners on the way home may be asking too much. The mental activity and the pressures of the husband's day may cause quite a bit of interference. The same request made before the husband starts a relaxing day at the pool may be an entirely different matter.

Let's assume we have a meeting scheduled with an associate during which a number of matters will have to be discussed. If we are honest with ourselves, we will face the fact that some of what's discussed will be forgotten, especially if it requires intense thought or involves strong emotions. Considering the interference theory, it would be better to first take up routine or noncontroversial matters and leave the more difficult items for later. Otherwise, it is possible to become so involved in debate that the noncontroversial matters may be totally omitted from the agenda.

Whenever situations arise in which we need to remember something such as numbers or terms, we should ask ourselves what type of mental activity will follow, and we should bear in mind that the more alike the intervening activity is to what we want to remember, the more will be forgotten. A wasteful amount of forgetting occurs during a normal business day precisely because this principle is not taken into account.

When We Forget

It appears that there is an actual physiological difference between what may be called *long-term memory* and *short-term memory*. We seem to recall remote experiences from childhood more readily than what occurred just a day ago. If, however, an experience has involved some special emotion, or person, or has been of particular significance, we have less difficulty remembering it.

In this connection the phenomenon of retrograde amnesia is interesting. A person may lose consciousness when he receives an unusually hard blow on the head or sustains a traumatic brain injury. When that person regains consciousness, it is very likely that he will be unable to recall what happened just prior to his losing consciousness. During recovery, events further away from the time of the injury are recalled first, and as recovery continues, events closer in time to the accident are recalled. In severe injury, there is often permanent loss of memory concerning what happened immediately preceding the injury.

It would seem that some sort of mental process requiring time is necessary for events to be stored, or consolidated, in long-term memory. Electroconvulsive shocks administered to the temples of monkeys a few minutes after they have learned a maze produce significant loss of recall, but such shocks given an hour or more later have little effect. These and similar observations are the basis of the theory of consolidation.

Generally, we do most of our forgetting shortly after learning. Items such as phone numbers, dates, names, and isolated facts are often forgotten in seconds unless we move them into our long-term memory shortly after we acquire them.

Implications of the Consolidation Theory

In business or social situations the learning of facts or dates may be followed by unrelated mental activity. Often, forgetting can be avoided by a quick review before undertaking another mental activity. It is usually best to review immediately, but when a large body of material is involved, it may be advisable to review an hour or so afterward. This is because often recall is better about one hour after learning than immediately afterward. This phenomenon is called *reminiscense*, which may be explained by the *serial position effect*. This phenomenon shows that after learning any list or body of information, memory will be better for the first and last items we learn. Thus, immediately following a lecture, memory may be good only for the beginning and end. However, after an hour or so, one can look back and get an overall view.

"Long" and "short" are relative terms used by psychologists to simplify a phenomenon. The brain itself makes no such distinction. Subjects under hypnosis have been able to recall extremely remote and trivial experiences — experiences that we would classify as being of short-term duration. This suggests the probability that consolidation is a matter of degree. There is no clear and sharp dividing line.

There is, however, a reason why the mind selects certain information for long-term memory and others are kept in memory for only a short time. Suppose someone says, "That man sitting down, the one in the middle, is the father of the girl who is playing the lead role tonight." Without short-term memory, we would forget the subject of the sentence. We would not remember who the person was talking about and we would be totally unable to carry on a conversation. Also, we would be unable to remember where we had just placed things or keep track of our ordinary daily activities. We would, in short, be in a hopeless predicament. Short-term memory acts as a kind of filter system. While most of our memories are short term, those that have had some special significance, or are related to some strong emotion, are generally stored in our long-term memory. When this occurs, we say our experiences have been consolidated.

Our Mental State During Recall

We have seen that the intensity of mental activity increases interference and makes forgetting more likely to occur later on. Tension and excitement will also be a powerful factor in forgetting if they are present at the exact time of recall. Obviously! Yet we often do not modify our learning habits to take this factor into account. Usually an individual will spend the same amount of time in preparing material whether it be for a lecture or for a debate. Yet should he prepare better for the former or the latter? Of course, the debate or argument would require more preparation. It is a matter of asking yourself, "What will my mental state be at the time when I will be expected to recall this information? What will the circumstances be?

Will it be under formal or informal conditions? Will it be friendly or hostile?" These and similar questions can help determine the tension level of the recall situation and you should then take more precise steps.

A young man in his early twenties revealed this interesting but not so unusual social problem. It seemed that often he would date a girl and the relationship would progress to the romantic stage. At that time he would say something to fit the mood, they would embrace, and then he would say, "Oh, I really go for you ..." And then blank! He had forgotten her name.

"Naturally," I told him, "consider your mental and emotional state at time of recall and just review that girl's name a little better than you would that of some more casual acquaintance."

Summary

This chapter discusses several conditions that effect memory. The passage of time is not the main factor in forgetting, rather it is the intensity and type of mental activity that we engage in between learning and recall, as well as our mental state during recall.

There are times, however, when we do the most forgetting. Generally, we do the most forgetting immediately after learning. Once information is retained over a period of time, it tends to be forgotten only gradually. Remembering these principles will improve our own memories and enable us to recognize that this is a factor we have to deal with when we interact with others.

Chapter Two

THE BASIC PRINCIPLES OF MEMORY
AND CONCENTRATION

Principle 1 — Organization and Memory

Suppose we are asked to remember these six words in order: *all, those, are, the, seat, car.* Foreseeing a little difficulty, we will repeat the words to ourselves to make sure that we have them firmly in mind. Now, suppose we add a few more words: *all, those, apples, are, in, the, back, seat, of, the, car.* Obviously, the second group is easier to remember, despite the fact that there are more words. The reason is that the second group makes sense; the words are organized into a meaningful pattern. If we should add the word *gravity* to the list, it would very likely be forgotten, since it does not fit into the structure. However, if we should add the word *blue*, it could very easily be inserted in front of the word *car.*

Psychological studies on the development of attitudes have shown that people will remember more of an argument if they agree with it. A group of students was divided into two groups: those considered pro-Communist and those considered anti-Communist. After hearing two speeches, pro and con, the students were asked questions about them. It was found that the two groups remembered more of the speech that was in accord with their own views. We might partially explain this in terms of motivation and interest, but most of the difference in remembering is due to differences in mental organization. The students remembered the ideas that could most easily be fitted into patterns that were already familiar to them.

We have pointed out that similarity of interpolated material affects recall adversely, and also that related information does not appreciably cause forgetting. Does this

11

seem like a contradiction? Let's try to clarify this with a further illustration. We are asked to go to the store to get these items, and we attempt to remember them without writing them down: *milk, eggs, bread, beans, soup, pork chops,* and *lettuce.* We review the list several times; then just as we are about to leave, we are given another list instead.

The new list contains: *butter, tuna fish, chopped meat,* and *raisins.* Because of interference, it would certainly be difficult to learn both lists. However, suppose instead of grocery items in our second list, we use other information, such as two containers, one dozen, two loaves, one can of, and so on, to a total of nine items of information. Would this list be difficult to remember? Certainly not, if we relate the two lists.

Now we can take in all the information by remembering two containers of milk, one dozen eggs, etc. In this case, there is no interference. *Two containers* has a quantitative relation to milk. The two items actually support each other; they have organization.

Finding and Creating Organization

Which figure is easier to produce from memory: *A* or *B*?

Fig. A   Fig. B

Of course *A* is easier, because it is organized into a distinctive, recognizable pattern. Figure *B* is difficult, but if we look closer, we can detect the organization there too. The first two lines on the left of figure *B* have no smaller line between them. Between the big lines the smaller lines increase in number from 0 to 3, while it can also be seen that each of the smaller lines increases in size.

Now we can reproduce figure *B* easily. What have we done? The figure did not change, rather our own perception of the pattern changed. When a person can perceive or recognize relationships, memory is enhanced.

Organization Depends on Our Perceptions

Our memory is a complex of interwoven systems and structures. All knowledge must relate to some other knowledge. If knowledge cannot find such a relationship, it will usually be discarded. This is why nonsense words are far more difficult to remember than words that have meaning and with which we are familiar. A new subject should therefore be approached with the aim of first learning its most basic concepts in order to form a frame of reference for additional knowledge.

Below is a square containing sixteen numbers. Memorize the square so that you can reproduce each number in its proper place:

4	2	1	0
2	6	5	7
7	5	6	9
0	1	4	8

A ... B ... D ... C

Does this seem like a difficult task? You might try to memorize each of the four rows separately. This would require several minutes of concentrated effort. Perhaps the technique you might use is repetition — simply repeat the numbers to yourself. This is the method most people use to remember things.

Suppose we try an easier approach and look for a semblance of organization. Let's mentally divide the square into four smaller squares. We will note that square *A* contains all even numbers in an arithmetic progression (i.e., 2, 4, 6). Squares B and D are easy to remember because they each contain the series 0, 1, 5, 7. Square C presents a problem, but if we look closely, we can find a relationship in the numbers. Now we solidify the relationship by noting the two diagonals: $A - C$ has all even numbers, and the two 6s are midway between 4 and 8; $B - D$ begins and ends with 0 and has 5s in the middle. If you will reread this paragraph once while referring to the square, you will, on completion, be able to reproduce the numbers exactly. Try it and see — but don't forget to visualize the entire square.

The superiority of the organization method over sheer repetition would be demonstrated if you were presented with additional squares to memorize. A second square would cause considerable interference with the first. There would be too many numbers. A third square would cause total breakdown unless a mnemonic association method (see pages 24-25) were used. The organization method, however, would not cause as much interference because the numbers would fit into larger patterns.

The organization method is particularly applicable to remembering telephone numbers. For example, in the number 639-2638, you will notice how the number 3 relates; then, numbers 6, 3, and 9 are multiples of 3; then noting the right side, two times 3 equals 6, minus 3 equals 3; and finally you note that the first two digits 2 and 6, add up to 8. There are other and perhaps better ways of remembering numbers, and these will be considered later. But for now, try to remember numbers through relationships and you will acquire a good insight into the principle of organization.

In the above instances, we were finding and creating organization where none existed. As long as our minds can perceive relationships, we will be able to remember. Fortunately, we do not always have to go through such maneuvers to find organization. It is usually made evident in a common-sense arrangement, though we do not always recognize or appreciate it.

Thought Structure in Daily Communication

Imagine yourself walking down a street and meeting your friend Bill. After exchanging greetings and a few casual words, Bill asks if you will be seeing a mutual friend named Tom. You answer yes, and Bill then asks you to do him a favor. "Sure, what is it?" you say. "Well, tell Tom that I won't be able to play golf with him tomorrow afternoon. I've heard the weather report and a bad storm is expected. It's nice weather now, but there's this storm up north, and the wind is blowing southward, which means we will get it tomorrow. Besides, last week I stepped in a ditch and twisted my ankle. I nearly broke my neck on that rotten course. It's still not fully healed."

It would be unreasonable for Bill to expect you to repeat his words exactly. Usually, we would transmit the message in one sentence. Which sentence would best convey the message?

Tom says:

   a. It's nice weather now and he nearly broke his neck on that rotten course.

   b. There's a storm up north.

   c. His ankle is still not healed.

   d. He can't play golf tomorrow.

Obviously, *d* is the best answer, even though it contains the least number of words. This answer is the core of the message, its main theme. If you do not remember the theme, you will not remember the message. It would be even better to add the two main ideas that Bill's ankle is still not healed and that there is a prospect of bad weather. In this case the message would be, "He can't play golf tomorrow because his ankle is still not healed and the weather is supposed to be bad."

"The wind is blowing southward" is a detail, and like any detail it is meaningless and easily forgotten unless it is associated with a main idea. In this case it is teamed up with the detail of "a storm up north," which is the main idea of prospective bad weather. "Bad weather" is the parent idea of the message, "can't play" is the grandparent, and "stepped in a ditch" is a cousin. The total information in the message forms a structure.

Is it too obvious to say that we should remember thoughts, not words? Suppose we ask someone if he remembers the Gettysburg Address. Person *A* says, "Yes, I remember that Lincoln said, 'Four score and seven years ago our forefathers brough forth this nation,' and that . . . oh yes, 'we could not consecrate or hallow this ground,' and the best part of all . . . 'the world will little note nor long remember what we say here, but it can never forget what they did here,' and 'that this nation was of the people, and by the people.' " Person *B* says, I don't remember the exact words, but he said that the nation was founded on great moral principles and that the people must be determined not to let it perish."

Of the two answers, it is *B* who can claim to have remembered the speech. Although he was unable to quote verbatim, he conveyed the essentials of the speech. Memory is best when we are able to recall the main theme of what we have read.

Principle 2 — Serial Reconstruction and Memory

As the examples of Bill's message and the Gettysburg Address will demonstrate, certain statements are more important than others because they remind us of other statements or facts that are related to them. We are familiar with the phenomenon of remembering called *serial reconstruction*. Something in the present causes us to remember an experience in the past; that experience brings to mind another experience closely associated with it; and that in turn recalls still another experience. The recall process can go on and on through a seemingly endless chain of events.

From this we can deduce that nothing is ever recalled by itself or without a reason. Any recollection comes about because it is triggered. Many memory techniques are derived from this principle. Often the key to memory lies in finding the one starting point, or one idea, that will trigger other related memories.

Yes, statements are capable of triggering other statements, but their effectiveness depends on their relative position in the total scheme. To remember that Bill said, "The weather is nice now" will be of little help in recalling the rest of the message. But if we first remember the main idea — that Bill can't play golf tomorrow — the logical recollection of *why* he can't play golf will more than likely come to mind. After the prospective storm and the bad ankle are remembered, it is then easier to remember how the ankle was injured, and why he feels there will be bad weather.

As for the Gettysburg Address, recalling the main theme of the speech will tend to trigger the essential points — assuming that the essential points were learned and understood previously, and not simply memorized as words. Furthermore, note how the main theme — that the people must not allow this great nation to perish — serves to recall other important parts of the speech, such as the political climate at the time. It is then easy to recall why Lincoln delivered the speech and the circumstances under which he delivered it.

Principle 3 — Discrimination and Memory

We have seen that certain ideas convey more information than other ideas. We have also seen that certain ideas, when properly organized, are more likely to recall related ideas. It becomes apparent that words and sentences vary tremendously in value. They may occupy the same space on paper but not in our minds.

All memory is selective. If you doubt this, ask yourself these questions: How many times have you seen a twenty dollar bill? Whose picture is on it? How many times have you picked up the telephone receiver and dialed the letter N? What number is in the same space as N? If these are difficult questions to answer, it is because the face and number were not selected for special attention.

Very likely *discrimination* is the most important principle in relation to memory. Any situation involving memory requires us, initially, to decide what is outstanding or unusual or important about it. Just undergoing the process of selecting the more important ideas or objects helps concentration and memory, as the following story demonstrates.

Here you are parking your car at the airport, and since you are applying the principles laid down in Chapter I, you know that the intensity of the situation (your hurry) may cause you to forget where you parked your car when you return. Telling yourself that you have parked your car in row 10, position B, is a lot better than just hurrying off. However, if you can pick out some landmark — a flagpole, a statue, or the like — and note where your car is in relation to it, you will remember. To recall, you will first ask yourself what you picked for a reminder, and your selection will always come back. Always make sure you choose a permanent landmark, or you'll find yourself looking for the Rolls Royce near where you think you parked. So much of having a good memory involves the crucial matter of finding that first starting point that will trigger related memories.

Extracting Concepts

Organization and discrimination can be used to commit certain things to memory by extracting a principle, or idea, or rule from a body of information. In studying the amendments to the Constitution of the United States, it is helpful to note such groupings as amendments 5 through 8 are about the courts and the jury system; amendments 9 through 11 deal with constitutional rights and the exercise of judicial power. If all the main points in a speech begin with a question, it would be well to note this in recalling the speech. You may recall the rule "*i* before *e* except after *c*" and let it help you to spell a word correctly.

Discrimination and Remembering Things to Do

We forget things we intend to do partly because we don't discriminate as to their relative importance. All intentions, all activities, such as writing a letter, answering an advertisement, undertaking an assignment, are related to our daily lives. One single task may be most urgent on a particular day and not on another. For proper recall, however, it isn't enough to recognize a relative difference or importance — mental attention must be directed to the nature of the difference. The best way to do this is to list things to do in the order of their importance and then to relate them to *when* they have to be done.

Principle 4 — Classification and Memory

Consider another type of organization. Suppose we need to remember these nine words in any order: *ranch, chair, legs, airplane, colonial, bed, duplex, car, rug*. This is considerably more difficult than the lists given at the beginning of this chapter. Nevertheless, we will try to remember them — only we will *classify* them under appropriate headings:

Types of Houses	Found in a House	Used for Transportation
ranch	chair	legs
colonial	bed	airplane
duplex	rug	car

Now remembering looks easier, doesn't it? Because we have classified the words, we have, in a sense, only three instead of nine items to recall, each one of which will make it easier to recall the words related to it.

Items that do not fit into an organized pattern will be more difficult to remember. If we add *hill, begin,* and *graph* to the above list, it will be more difficult to remember, because these words do not fit into any of the categories we established.

The principle we're concerned with is this: *The smaller the unit or category, the easier it will be to recall its components.* Let's see how this principle operates with the principle of discrimination discussed earlier in this chapter.

A lieutenant in the fire department has just been transferred, and his first job is to memorize the fastest route to any location in his district. With the report of a blazing fire before him it would certainly be embarrassing to start consulting a map. The fireman makes his job of memorizing easier in the following way: (1) he divides the district into six areas; (2) he selects one landmark from each area — a place which he knows he can reach without delay, and which is located near the center of each area; (3) then he memorizes each street in relation to the landmark in each area. Isn't this a lot easier than trying to remember each street in relation to the fire station? Common sense? Yes, of course — but we must never miss an opportunity to divide, classify, or categorize.

Principle 5 — Applied Imagination and Memory

In dealing with information, the mind handles visual images, sound, and linguistic and tactile memories. Increasingly, modern man relies on language, or verbalization, as a source of memory. A person who is asked what he did yesterday will most likely reply, "I went to the opera," or "I typed a report." The actual image of going to the opera, or typing a report will not be evoked.

Members of primitive tribes have been known to be very skillful in parlor games which require the ability to remember pictures. Those of a tribe who have been educated, however, are not as skillful. Apparently, modern communication fosters verbal ability, possibly at the expense of visual ability. In today's world, if the ability to remember through visual images seems to lessen with age, it is because we use the verbal faculty more than we use the image faculty, and not because of age per se.

We should not, therefore, underrate the value of visualization memory. It is a faculty we are born with. Parents of a one-year-old infant learning to feed himself have observed this: The infant does not say to himself, "Okay, first I must reach out my arm, then I grab the food, then bend my elbow, then open my mouth for it . . ." It is more likely that the infant has a picture of the procedure in his mind.

Visual memory is more lasting than verbal memory. Which would stay with you longer: a glimpse of a face or a name that takes a second to say? The face, of course. In more instances than we realize, visualizing details and events is the best way to remember and is therefore an important factor in memory improvement.

Later in this book we will introduce some exercises that will help you to start thinking in visual terms and give you practice in visualizing. Meanwhile, we offer the following basic suggestions:

1. Make sure you imagine everything clearly and in vivid colors. We tend to remember a gaily-colored image better than one in white, black, or gray.

2. Don't be afraid to exaggerate. We tend to imagine things their actual size. You will remember better if you make things larger.

3. Try to see everything in three dimensions (length, breadth, depth) instead of in the usual two dimensions (length and breadth).

4. Always visualize in movement and action — they are easier to remember than "still" pictures.

Principle 6 — Ego Involvement and Memory

Now we come to the principle of personal involvement which means that we are much better at remembering things about ourselves than about others. With this in mind, try to commit the following essay to memory, using the visualization principle and the principle of personal involvement. If you find a place for yourself in the essay, if you visualize the description in three dimensions and in vivid color, and if you exaggerate, you will be amazed at how well you can recall the directions and facts concerning Venus. Try it!

VENUS OBSERVED

NASA's Mariner II spacecraft flew past Venus at a distance of 21,648 miles, giving man his first relatively close observation of Earth's mysterious planetary neighbor. This Venus fly-by climaxed an epic spaceflight experiment that significantly advanced the world's knowledge about Venus and about interplanetary space while contributing to the planning for man's eventual journeys to the Moon and other planets.

The Mariner observations, together with radar and optical studies made from Earth, caused man to discard any romantic notions that may have persisted of Venus as a place with earthlike qualities. Mariner found that the temperatures of Venus may be as hot as 800° F. This temperature, hot enough to melt lead, precluded the possibility of life like that on Earth.

Radar studies provide evidence that Venus rotates once each 225 Earth days, while orbiting the Sun in the same time period. Thus, each day or night on Venus lasts about 112½ Earth days, or half the planet's rotational period. Presumably clouds screen out most of the sunlight, keeping that hemisphere in twilight.

Because of the long Venusian day and night, man expected the side facing the sun to be quite hot and the other side very cold. Mariner II, however, did not find any appreciable difference in temperature, so the dense atmosphere must circulate vast quantities of heat from the day side to the night side.

———————————

I hope you placed yourself in the spacecraft and really felt the heat and visualized the action and color — all in three dimension. If you did, it will certainly be a long time before you forget these facts about Venus.

Here is another exercise. Imagine you are lost and stop at a gas station for directions. The attendant says, "Oh sure, no problem. Just go up three blocks, turn right, and go straight for six traffic lights. Then turn left. You will come to a fork, where you will bear right and go over a bridge. Then go two blocks, make a left turn, and you'll see the building you are looking for on your left. You can't miss it."

Relying on your memory of these directions, make a rough sketch. If you think you missed some of the directions while visualizing them in the sketch, you can try again. Or, you can just say to yourself, "I'll go up three blocks, turn right, and then ask someone else." Best of all from what you have learned so far about visualization and ego involvement, you should be able to put yourself in the driver's seat. As you see yourself in action, turning the wheel and re-creating the whole experience, you will remember more and more of the directions.

Principle 7 — Emotions and Memory

Happenings that are charged with emotion have a way of staying in our memory. For example, those who are old enough to remember the shock of President Kennedy's assassination are able to recall not only the event and the surrounding atmosphere, but also their own feelings. Emotions will very often evoke other emotions and they in turn will recall memories that are associated with them.

Principle 8 — Association and Memory

In recalling the breakfast you ate this morning, you are also able to recall those who were at the table with you. This image may remind you of a task you must perform. Impressions are not stored in the brain and then recalled in an isolated state. They are more or less related, and recall takes place through association with other impressions. It stands to reason that the more connections or associations there are, the more easily recall will occur. We can state this in a principle: *Memory improvement consists, to a large extent, of increasing the number and closeness of associations.*

Ideas combine in all sorts of ways. There are such familiar associations as *cup* and *saucer*, or such time and place associations as *thunder* and *lightning*. Things become associated through similarity in meaning, such as *house* and *home*, or through similarity of sound, such as *bought* and *taught*. There is even association through opposites, such as *hot* and *cold*, *tall* and *short*. Then there is association of cause and effect. We step on the brake to avoid an accident and the car slows down. The brake is the cause and the slowdown is the effect. There are whole and part associations, such as *tub* and *bathroom*, *library* and *books*. And finally there are associations through similarity of form or class, such as *lion, tiger, leopard*.

Here is a list of words and numbers that are associated:

one	ton
two	feet
three	tree
four	aft
five	fingers
six	shooter
seven	dice
eight	ate
nine	cat lives
ten	toes

Two, five, and *ten* are associated in place. *Seven* is associated for the same reason, but it is slightly less familiar. The combinations with *one* and *three* rhyme. *Four* is associated because *fore* and *aft* are opposites on a ship. *Six* and *shooter* form a whole-part relationship through the idea of a pistol. *Eight* and *ate* are homonyms; and *nine* and the lives of a cat are very familiar associations. Simple associations can be memorized very quickly to aid memory.

Mnemonics and Cues as Associations

There are instances when it is difficult to establish an association. We cannot, for example, link *eight* or *eighth* with Martin Van Buren, the eighth President of the United States. Nor can we link the French word *manger* with its meaning, "to eat." In such instances we can use our own ingenuity to contrive a device or system that will help us associate and remember. These systems or devices are known as *mnemonics.*

Closely related to mnemonics are *cues.* Whenever remembering one thing serves to recall another, the idea or object that helps us recall is called the *cue.* In other words, when someone says *five,* we often spontaneously think of *fingers.* The cue association mechanism works backward too: the word *fingers* may recall the number *five* to us.

One curious aspect of cues is that they can be substituted and simulated. The word *aft,* for example, can be cued with *fore,* while at the same time we can think of the number *four*. This is also true of *eat* and *ate,* which can at the same time evoke the number *eight*. A sort of mental transposittion occurs in these instances, a process about which we know very little at present.

Using Mnemonics and Cues in Verbal Associations

We are now going to memorize the meanings of the words below by making use of mnemonics and cues:

savant	boulanger
tengo	livre
cibus	lambent
bumptious	château
acrimonious	risa

Where an association between a particular word and its meaning does not exist offhand, it is our job to make one, somehow. For example, you may find that a new or foreign word sounds like another word with which you are familiar. The familiar word may be close enough in meaning to remind you of the foreign word. The word *savant* in French means "a wise man, an expert." It is easy to see how similar it is to two expressions you are probably familiar with: *savvy* (smart) and *savoir faire* (having social knowledge or poise).

Many words can be associated verbally, by using them in a sentence that carries the meaning. The Spanish word *tengo* and its meaning "I have" can be the basis of a sentence like *I have tengo* (to go).

A concrete word is one that can be pictured. *Cat* and *rock* are examples of concrete, easily visualized words. Words that are concepts, like *truth, confidence,* and *justice,* are examples of abstract words, and they cannot be visualized. You will find that a verbal association can be used to advantage when a word is too abstract for visual association.

Visual Associations

Lambent is an adjective meaning "brilliant, radiant." We must link the word and its meaning somehow. Let's look at the word and see if we can find another word within it, which we can use as our cue. We find the word *lamb*. We can now visualize a lamb of shining and radiant brilliance. Later on, when we want to recall the meaning of *lambent*, we will think of the word *lamb* and visualize it, and then notice that bright, shiny, and radiant are associated with it.

We used a visual cue to associate the word *lambent* with its meaning. Association can be visual or verbal, but the visual tends to be longer lasting than the verbal, as stated in Principle 5.

Now let's consider the Latin word *cibus*, meaning "food." In it we find the word *bus*. Then we picture a bus stuffed and overflowing with food. Make your association large and in vivid colors. Absurd? But we won't forget the meaning. What more could we ask for?

The word *acrimonious* is an adjective meaning "sharp, biting," as in a remark. Look again and you will see the word *rim* in it. Then visualize a rim, one that is extremely sharp. *Bumptious* means "confident and blustering." Can you picture a very confident *bum*? Of course you can — your mind can do anything. *Boulanger* means "baker" in French. Visualize a baker in a rage. Also, note that *boulanger* and *baker* both begin with the letter *b*.

Now we come to the word *livre*, the French word for "book." Try to do it yourself: picture a book with liver in it. You are well on your way to excellent visual association if you can. Let's be clear about this: Logic, or lack of it, is no factor in determining visual association. Indeed, sometimes the more absurd your association, the better you will be able to remember. The important factor in visual association is the clarity with which you visualize something in your own mind. The sooner you discard your inhibitions, the better will be your skill at visual association.

Backward Association

Usually, when you associate a word you would think of the word first and then connect it to its meaning. Taking the Spanish word *risa*, which means "laughter," you might picture yourself rising as a result of laughter. Later, if you needed to recall the meaning of the word, you would easily recall it by first recognizing the letters *r-i-s*. However, suppose you are given the word *laughter* and you want to recall its Spanish equivalent. Now you must recall the association backwards, and that is somewhat more difficult. You must think of *laughter* and that should recall *rising*, which should lead you to *risa*. Although this method of backward association may pose problems, it is still a vast improvement over sheer rote memory.

Let's take *château*, the French word for "castle," and associate it visually. You think of a castle and your vision produces it in the shape of a *hat*. (Notice that you chose *hat* from the word *château* as your cue.) Later on, in recall, when you visualize a castle, you will have the hint that the desired word has *hat* in it, and then you should be able to remember the word *château*. A visual, backward association will usually bring to mind some other word that is closely related to it.

Let's review the meanings of the following words: *livre, bumptious, lambent, acrimonious,* and *cibus*. If you have studied and grasped the idea of visual and backward association, you will be able to commit to memory not only foreign words and technical terms, but you will be able to retain any fact or idea and recall it at will. Here is a basic procedure that will be of further help in associating and remembering:

1. Decide on your subject: a person, object, word, thought, or activity.

2. Pick out (discriminate) something from the subject that you have decided on. Your selection could be something unique or something that is familiar, such as *bus* in *cibus*.

3. Using cues when necessary, associate your selection with whatever you wish to remember about your subject.

4. To aid in recall, ask yourself what you picked out about the subject (person, object, word, thought, or activity) that is associated with your selection. What you picked out will be your cue to associating and remembering.

If the above is not entirely clear, don't worry. Association techniques are dealt with several times in this book, and you will have plenty of opportunity to increase your knowledge and understanding.

The Techniques of Chaining

One value of association is that it can always be "chained" to another association so that any number of ideas can be triggered by one initial thought.

Suppose, for example, you wanted to memorize the principles of memory improvement in the exact order that you have studied them. You begin by telling yourself a story, the cues for which relate to the principles of memory. Picture yourself as a prince (cue for basic principles), sitting down to play the organ (cue for organization). Your cereal (serial reconstruction) is brought to you on a disc (discrimination). The rest of your memory effort involves classification, imagination, ego involvement, emotion, and association. Continue with more of the story, and then see if you can remember all eight principles by relating them to your visual chain.

Visualization, Association, and the Reduction of Stress

There may be an added benefit in converting information from the complex and abstract to the concrete and familiar, and then chaining the visualizations in a story. If we are excited, frightened, or angry, there is a corresponding reaction in many, if not all, areas of our bodies. It has been shown that the manner in which we deal with information can add to or detract from the amount of stress we undergo. The world in which we live makes so many abstract demands on us, that in our attempt to cope with these demands, we tend to overuse our verbal skill at the sacrifice of our visual skill. We use words to remember, we talk with words, we think with words, and we communicate with words. This overloading of our verbal capacity, at the expense of the visual, may be a source of tension. Perhaps the overuse of our verbal sense explains the increasing popularity of *meditation* — an activity which is, basically, an extended, intense, visual effort.

Even our daydreams are visual extensions of the psyche. They are regarded as desirable psychologically. This is also true of our dreams at night. A person who is consistently awakened during a dream will often evince the familiar symptoms of tension.

Although at this writing the science of psychology is not sure how or why we dream, it is suspected that dreams may help to balance the activities of the brain. Whether this is true or not, it does seem that handling more material visually rather than verbally is beneficial.

If we bear this in mind, we can find many more opportunities to visualize our experiences. How often have we started to make a list of groceries and repeated the items to ourselves verbally? We could just as easily visualize the items, or visualize ourselves selecting the items from the shelves. By doing this we can take some of the burden away from the verbal area.

Can the visual area be overused as much as we overuse the verbal? It does not appear so. It seems that our ability to imagine is boundless and is not as subject to the interference discussed in Chapter I. As long as we do not limit our imaginations, we can make great use of visual association.

Principle 9 — Differences in Memory

Thus far we have seen that one idea, statement, fact, experience, place, or object can serve to recall one or more different facts, ideas, places, experiences or objects. So much of memory improvement depends upon finding that one starting point, that first recollection, that will start other memories rolling back.

We have also noted that some ideas readily recall other ideas stored in the memory. That which is unique, unusual, absurd, extraordinary, or just plain different from your own pattern of experience will often serve as an excellent starting point because your attention, both in learning and recall, will be drawn to the difference.

Suppose, for example, you are shown five houses and their interiors. The outside of four of the houses is painted in dark colors; the fifth house is painted pink. If all other factors were equal, the pink house would more likely be remembered before the other houses. The unusual idea of a pink house would also serve to recall its interior before we recalled the interiors of the other houses.

Part of the technique of recalling information about a subject, topic, person, object, or place lies in first asking yourself what you "picked out." If your selection was something unusual, it would be more readily recalled, particularly if you associated other ideas with the outstanding feature. This concept will be quite helpful in remembering facts.

Two more key points are relevant here. One is that not only does noting the difference help memory, but just looking for that which is unique, prominent, or extraordinary greatly helps too; the second is that when you use your imagination to create associations, it will often be of greater help to you if you make your images unusual.

Principle 10 — Motivation, Goal Setting and Memory

Several years ago a young woman told me about her husband, who apparently had a fine memory for matters pertaining to his occupation but was hopelessly forgetful about little things around the house. As a matter of professional interest, I gave the husband a list of mnemonic associations for numbers. (We will learn about these later.) After a few hours of practice, he confidently announced to his wife that he could remember forty things to get from the store without a list. Not too convinced, she tested her husband, writing down the items as she called them out. Sure enough, the husband recalled all forty items in the exact order of the list. The wife thought the feat was superhuman and that her troubles were over.

Wait. This is not the end of the story. The husband left the house to go to the store and purchase the forty items. When he returned, he had forgotten only one thing — to go to the store!

Any one of us could be that young man. We constantly forget unpleasant things: obligations, dental appointments, bills, and so on. We rarely forget a task that is pleasant. We remember subjects that are interesting and forget those we find boring. As we said earlier, we are more apt to remember points in an argument if they are in accord with our own beliefs.

It would seem that part of the trouble in the situation of the husband and wife has to do with motivation. The man was motivated to remember the forty items when challenged, but despite good intentions, he was not too concerned with going to the store.

Concentration requires the expenditure of energy. Motivation and interest are the fuel behind that energy. There is hardly any limit to what a human being can achieve if he is sufficiently motivated. Interest is a major factor in learning and memory. Hence, any suggestions that will help secure it, even in a small degree, are worthwhile. The suggestions discussed next can be undertaken with very little effort.

Setting Goals

A goal is a measurable level of performance toward which a person may strive. Examples of goals are obtaining a promotion, getting married, and finishing an assignment. As you can see, goals can be long range or short range.

Goal setting is important for many different reasons. Books have been written telling people how to succeed, how to think, how to get rich, how to be happy — the subjects are endless. The central theme of many of these books is the value of setting and working towards a goal. If you are determined in your desire to become a physician, a scientist, or a lawyer, for example, you are more likely to be interested in your work than someone who lacks a definite goal. This is true of everyone, regardless of age. Once you have set up an objective, the intermediate steps become more interesting because they are seen clearly as steps leading toward a desired result.

We have seen that memory and organization are integrally related. Goal setting is also related to organization in a larger sense, and to the function of memory. It is no accident that people who are extremely forgetful will also tend to describe themselves as disorganized, especially about everyday affairs. Perhaps they lack a sense of continuity in their lives. Little things that need doing are regarded as without purpose. Chores are not performed with a goal in mind. A typical example is the college student who habitually fails to do his homework assignments. The student swears that his failure to do them was unintentional and that he would have done them if only he had remembered. Usually, this attitude can be traced to the student's own admission that he does not know why he is going to school, or what he wants to do after he graduates.

Setting Short-Range Goals

It is well known that a person will concentrate better when he has a goal in mind. What is somewhat less well known is that performance and effort increase as a person nears his goal. An exhausted cross-country runner often gets a second wind as he nears the finish line.

If, let us say, you have 100 pages to read, it may appear as quite a task. If, however, you were to divide the assignment into smaller parts, you would increase the number of goals and thus would have more finish lines. You would then attain more levels of satisfaction since you would always be close to attaining a goal. Books and other printed matter are usually divided into chapters, headings, and subheadings, so that it isn't difficult to set short-range reading goals as you go along.

Finish What You Have Started

We have said that intensity of interference is a factor in forgetting, yet intensity is really dependent on the psychological makeup of the individual. The person who is bothered by worries or who always has troubled thoughts will bring these worries and thoughts to new situations. His own state of mind will cause more than normal interference. To a large extent, tension can be avoided by completing each task started.

One characteristic of projects, tasks, and obligations is that they are subject to interruptions by other matters. Some people have the habit of always putting a task aside to do other tasks, with the result that they almost never finish anything. Once a goal is established, particularly one that requires mental energy, it should be completed. Failure to complete a goal is not only an inefficient use of time, but it can also create a state of tension which can hamper a person and diminish his ability to perform other tasks. Failure to complete a task the night before will render a person more susceptible to distraction and forgetfulness the next morning. The completion of a task carries with it a measure of satisfaction that reduces tension and will help to raise the level of performance in other tasks.

Principle 11 — The Sound of Your Voice and Memory

It is amazing how we can be affected by the sound of our own voice. In one study, for example, individuals were selected at random and given a viewpoint to defend on a particular subject. Oddly enough, it was found that after the debate a debater's personal views had shifted toward those he had been assigned to defend.

It may sound a bit "off," but if you simply say out loud something like "I want to learn how the new machine works by reading this chapter," it will enhance your interest, increase your concentration, help you to remember, and give you the motivation to do so. Your brain listens to and remembers the sound of your voice. How often have you asked a friend to remind you of something? Your friend may forget, but you distinctly remember "voicing" the request.

To a large extent we can solve the problem of forgetting where we put things by saying, "I am now placing the voucher in the upper right-hand drawer," or "I am now placing the receipt in the glove compartment." Vocalizing will do wonders for recall and should be used whenever possible. A business schedule can often be planned and remembered while driving to work in the morning, if the planning has been verbalized out loud. Sometimes, on a rainy or foggy morning, you may want to turn the lights on in your car. To avoid the possibility of leaving the lights on, if you say out loud "I have just turned my lights on. I shall turn them off as soon as I turn off the motor," you won't forget to do it.

Man, because he is a social animal, needs to communicate with others. Discussions are usually more fun than lectures or reading by yourself because lively conversation is involved. Speech can readily transform drudgery into interest. The more you talk and discuss things, the greater will be your interest and your ability to remember.

Principle 12 — Your Actions and Memory

Just as we remember our own words and thoughts, so will we also remember our own actions. Body movements can often provide a starting point to trigger recall. You may have forgotten the contents of a lecture you attended some weeks ago, yet you can start a chain of memories by asking yourself if you raised a question during the lecture. If you remember the question, you will recall the answer, which will, in turn, recall the lecture. Usually, you can recall the question if you visualize the body movement of raising your hand.

Writing is also an aid to memory and concentration because here, too, body movement is involved. Blind people who regain their sight through an operation report that they still feel it is more effective to use braille to read because of the physical movement involved. When trying to recall where you placed something, try to recall the physical movement that went with it.

Principle 13 — Your Understanding and Memory

Some people can memorize a poem or a song or even a speech without the vaguest notion of its meaning. Most of us can recall such an experience from elementary school, when we had to learn things by rote. Very likely we could still memorize that way if we could duplicate the motivation. The chances are against it because meaning, use, and understanding take on more and more importance as we grow older.

It is easier to remember something that has meaning for us. As we mentioned earlier, nonsense words that have no particular meaning or relationship to other words are readily forgotten, while real, familiar words are not. Mathematical formulas are retained when we understand and know how to apply them.

Factors Influencing Comprehension

Learning and memory are enhanced when what we are learning has meaning for us. You may recall, in geometry, that the formula for the area of a triangle is found by multiplying the base times the height and dividing by two. It is no monumental feat to remember this, but when it is placed alongside other formulas — those for finding areas of rectangles, circles, other triangles, and parallelograms, as well as for circumferences and volumes — considerable interference can result. If, however, the elementary base times height of a rectangle is understood, the formula for the area of a triangle becomes more comprehensible. From figure C we can see that any right triangle is actually half of a rectangle; therefore, half the base times the height. Next we notice that no matter what the angles of the triangle may be, it will always fit into a rectangle. If it is not a right triangle, it will make two other triangles, see x and y in figure D, and their totals will equal the original triangle. Hence, the formula works for any triangle. The student who acquires an understanding of this will not forget the formula.

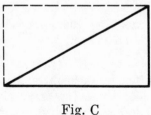
Fig. C

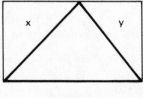
Fig. D

There are a great many factors — mental, emotional, and environmental — that affect our level of comprehension. A person may fail to understand something (a paragraph or a chapter) for a number of complex reasons. It would require a separate book to do justice to this subject. Nevertheless, because comprehension in learning is extremely important in retention, we will discuss it here briefly.

Prior Knowledge and Memory

The knowledge a person brings to a subject is probably the single most important factor in comprehension. We can say that prior knowledge is a prerequisite for the acquisition of new knowledge. This can be said about learning to repair a television. One can hardly undertake such a repair without a firm foundation in basic electronics.

While in most of the liberal arts prior knowledge is not absolutely essential, yet it certainly has a bearing on comprehension. All things being equal, someone who has a fair background in Greek history will be better able to comprehend a selection on Alexander the Great than someone who does not have such a background. The person who already has a frame of reference has an advantage in absorbing new information. Because of this, other aspects of Greek history will take on more meaning, and the newly acquired information will in turn be affected by the previously acquired information.

Acquisition of New Knowledge and Memory

We can see that organized structures in memory act like sponges. The larger these organized structures, the easier it is for new concepts to be absorbed. As we have said, memory depends to some extent on comprehension, and comprehension in turn depends on memory.

Memories are not always used to best advantage in acquiring new knowledge. They often lie dormant and are only slightly useful at a subconscious level. They may also be consciously activated. Two people may possess the same amount of knowledge about a subject, but the one who recalls and remembers more will have an advantage in understanding. It is evident, therefore, that before starting to learn something new about a subject, you should try to recall as much as possible of what you already know about it. By this means you prepare yourself to assimilate the new knowledge.

Principle 14 — Your Thoughts and Memory

Some very interesting observations relating to memory development can be made by watching young children. Factors that cause variations in adult memory performance also apply to children. Several years ago, my wife and I and my son (who was not quite two at the time) were having dinner at a friend's house. The dessert was a warm delicious brownie, to which the boy instantly took a liking. When he had eaten his brownie, he wanted another but didn't know how to ask for it, because he had not been told the name.

I became aware of his predicament when I felt him tugging at my arm and saying, "More chawkit bwed," while pointing to the far end of the table. At first, I didn't know what he wanted. Then it dawned on me. I said, "Oh, chocolate bread. Yes, that makes sense," and handed him another brownie. It wasn't until five months later that we had brownies again. Five months is a very long time in the life of a two-year-old. Yet when he saw the brownies, he immediately exclaimed with glee, "O-o-o, chawkit bwed!" He had not forgotten — quite a memory feat for his age.

Had we told the child that what he wanted was called a brownie, he most likely would not have remembered it. He remembered "chawkit bwed" because these were his own words, and they had meaning for him. They fitted into his own memory structure. *We are better able to remember our own thoughts than the thoughts of another.* Once we have solved a problem through our own conscious processes, we do not easily forget the problem or its solution.

Memory and concentration in reading technical material will be greatly helped by a little thought. We will go into this further in the chapter on reading. Meanwhile, let's see how thinking helps memory.

The location of an object can be recalled if you think before you put it down. Having a reason *why* an object ought to be in a particular drawer, and not in another, will assist recall. The thought, the reason, will be recalled, and you will then be able to remember the particular drawer.

Principle 15 — Your Health and Memory

This book offers you practically all you need to know about memory. If you follow the principles laid down and the techniques suggested — and if you use them creatively — you will have a far better memory than you had before, even if you wisely realize that like everybody else, you have your own limitations.

Stated simply, memory is the result of the complex interaction of brain cells. Oxygen is a necessary element in brain performance. When elderly people whose memory may be failing are given large amounts of oxygen, their ability to remember shows improvement and their retention span is longer. It is evident that poor body circulation results in an inadequate supply of oxygen being supplied to the brain, which results in lessened mental performance. The human circulatory system is also affected by what a person eats and drinks and the degree to which he is physically fit. Exercise is important to our physical and mental fitness and general well-being mostly because it increases circulatory activity. Clearly, good health is a factor in good mental functioning.

Principle 16 — Review and Memory

The more the brain deals with any given information, the better it will operate and retain the information. The principle and technique of review was dealt with briefly in the earlier discussion of long- and short-term memory. It will be considered again when we discuss reading and study skills. For now, it is important to realize that there are basically two forms of review: repetition and self recitation. In the former, you review the material over and over again by constant reference to it. In the latter, you also review, but without reference to the material. *Self-*

recitation is far superior to rote repetition in the effort to remember. The more you recite to yourself, without resorting to the material, the greater the ability to recall, as numerous experiments have demonstrated.

Principle 17 — Mental Preparation and Memory

When the brain is prepared for something that will happen in the future, it will function better, not only with regard to memory, but also with regard to relevant psychological aspects. Alvin Toffler, in his book *Future Shock*, has shown that anticipation and preparation for a future event helps to reduce stress and possible physiological harm. This principle relates to other suggestions made in this book such as goal setting, imagining a use, generating thoughts, and ascertaining difficulty in recall. The principle of mental preparation is so important however that it is being treated separately.

Has this ever happened to you? As a student, you did your homework and you knew the material you had studied. Suddenly, without warning, the teacher asked a question — you were at a loss for an answer and were faced with a problem of recall. Here is a suggestion. If you are absorbing information, and if you have reason to believe that you may be asked to recall it under tense circumstances (perhaps by a boss, by a teacher, or before an audience), prepare yourself for such a situation. Visually create the information and the answer in your mind as clearly as possible. Imagine the person or persons waiting impatiently for your answer. Then, imagine responding with the correct answer.

Principle 18 — Usage and Memory

It is well known that the human body is affected by the needs of the environment. A man who has engaged in physical work for years and suddenly finds himself at a desk job will probably lose some of the strength in his muscles unless he exercises them. There is no reason why brain cells should react differently. They must be kept in use, or forgetting will result.

Here we need to draw a distinction between usage and exercise. If a man, in chopping wood for fire, lifts an ax repeatedly, he is using his muscles. If he is using his muscles to lift weights, he is exercising. If a student repeats foreign phrases to himself in preparing for a test, he is exercising his memory. If he goes to a foreign country, he will be able to use the phrases.

Usage is the surest aid to retention. A bright college student may have some difficulty remembering the principles of insurance or investment in an economics course. But a young married man of average intelligence, who has a practical need for these principles, won't have such difficulty. In other words, he is in a position to put these principles to use.

Finding a Use

Even if you don't have an immediate need to use certain information you can and should imagine situations where you will have such a need. When you hear an anecdote, for example, you might think of a time and place where you can tell it. If you come upon something of interest that you have seen or read, imagine a conversation that would give you a chance to talk about it. Use your acquired knowledge at every opportunity, and don't forget to use the techniques you have learned in this book.

Summary

Having shown how a number of factors can work to aid memory and concentration, we are ready to say that they do not function by magic but through the application of principles and techniques — those dealt with in this chapter.

One concept is very clear: In order for your memory to function properly, you must use your mind. Your mind doesn't function by means of secret switches that are turned on and off. You must think about information; you must visualize, associate, organize, discriminate, vocalize, become personally involved, set goals, and review. *You yourself must do these things.* Don't think you can just relax and absorb information. Optimum learning — and remembering — is a creative act.

We should consider for a moment the problem of when and how to apply the principles and techniques you have been reading about. Obviously, you cannot apply all of them — for either one situation or for many. Frankly, there are no easy answers. Your own ability and your willingness to cooperate must be taken into account.

We have tried to show how certain principles affect mental functioning; we will, in the following chapter, undertake to show how these techniques and principles are used in some typical problem areas of memory. You will be shown how you can apply these techniques and principles, even beyond the particular examples that are given in this book.

Chapter Three

HOW TO READ FOR COMPREHENSION
AND RETENTION

One of the characteristics of the mind that relates to reading is that it thrives on what is best described as *meaning*. Sometimes when we hear words and more words, nothing sinks in. Suddenly, we grasp the ideas expressed by these words, and the words take on meaning. The word *a* and the word *red* together, for example, do not convey any meaning to us. If we add the word *apple*, we have a phrase that the brain can accept; *a red apple* has meaning.

Another characteristic of the mind is that it seems to thrive on activity during nonsleeping hours. In fact, it is almost impossible to keep the mind inactive and blank for any length of time. It is probably more difficult to have the mind go blank altogether than to keep it fixed in thought. We must always be thinking of something. Let's see how the two principles of meaning and activity can result in concentration while reading.

Establishing Good Reading Habits for Concentration

You have no doubt had the experience of reading a page, and halfway down suddenly realize that your mind has wandered. Poor reading habits can be corrected through instruction and practice in the principles of developmental reading. We will briefly consider the basic principles of reading as they apply to concentration.

The poor reader is apt to read one word at a time, and then repeat each word silently, so that meaning is absorbed at such a slow rate the brain becomes bored and distracted. When the reader with poor reading habits comes to the phrase "a red apple," the first focus is on the word *a*, which is repeated. Unfortunately, *a* doesn't mean anything to the brain. Then the poor reader will focus on *red*. Still no information has been transmitted to the brain, for the word *red*, even with the word *a*, means nothing unless it is associated with a word like *house*, or some other noun.

With good reading habits it is possible to take in an entire phrase at a glance. Instead of repeating each word separately, the image that the words represent enters the mind. Admittedly, breaking the habit of reading one word at a time and subvocalizing (repeating each word silently to oneself), isn't easy, but the acquisition of good reading habits results in improved reading skill and helps concentration.

Reading Faster for Concentration

When you have difficulty keeping your mind on what you are reading, it may be because your reading is so slow that you are vocalizing every *it, the, and,* and *to.* Comprehension will be lessened because you have to give so much attention to the physical act of saying the words. Slow reading does not necessarily help concentration. On the contrary, faster reading is more likely to improve it.

Suppose we give slow reading the benefit of the doubt and assume that you can attain the following scores in comprehending an article by using different methods. You may set out to read the article slowly, at perhaps 250 words a minute, and attain a comprehension score of 70 percent. Or you may read the article twice at 500 words per minute, and after the second reading you will once again score 70 percent. It would appear that reading fast would not gain an advantage. This is not true, however, because the slow way is so susceptible to distraction that even the goal of 250 words may not have been reached, and the actual count may not have been more than 150 words per minute.

Adjusting Your Reading Rate

We are not saying that you should always increase your reading speed. Actually, how fast you should read depends upon the difficulty of the material. Light fiction can doubtless be read five times faster than a technical article in a professional journal. There is some easy reading in every piece of reading matter — therefore you should be able to adjust your reading rate as you go along.

Many people suffer lapses of concentration in reading because they don't try to adjust their reading rate to the material. They make the mistake of reading easy and difficult material at the same rate. The objective should be to supply input to the brain at a rate that it can handle with understanding. A rate faster than this optimum level causes loss of comprehension; a rate slower causes mind-wandering.

Looking for Organization

When two or more people get together to try to accomplish something that neither can do separately, they have created an organization. Similarly, when letters are joined in a systematic fashion to form a word, the word is an organization that can transmit information which the letters separately cannot. Words are then organized to form a sentence. The sentences contribute to the formation of a paragraph. The paragraph is part of a broader organization.

Ideas, whether expressed in speaking or in writing, possess structure and organization. If we fail to perceive this organization while we are reading, we are inviting our mind to wander and we are hampering our ability to retain information.

Let's practice looking for organization while reading. We will start with the paragraph. Each paragraph contains one idea, even if it offers many facts, descriptions, words, or examples. Acquire the habit of looking for this one idea in a paragraph while reading. If you are in doubt as to what the one idea is, ask yourself this question, "If I wanted to convey the message in this paragraph, how would I express it?"

The Paragraph

1. The reason these little barnacles interest one so much is that they have a bad habit which costs

shipowners about $100,000,000 a year. When young, the barnacle swims and does no harm, but on reaching maturity, it attaches itself to something — a ship bottom, for instance — grows a shell and sticks there. Ships become so encrusted that they have to be laid up periodically for scraping and repainting.

Which statement comprises the main idea?

    a. The young barnacle does no harm.
    b. The mature barnacle grows a shell.
    c. Shipping is hindered by barnacles.
    d. Barnacles are interesting.

2. Scientists find that smoke from American cities shuts out from 3 to 50 percent of sunshine, with its health-giving rays. Inhalation of this smoke induces serious inflammatory and nerve disorders. Government recording instruments show that 30 percent more sunshine falls upon Governors Island in New York Bay, away from the city's smoke, than upon Manhattan Island.

Which statement comprises the main idea?

    a. Smoke shuts out health-giving sunshine.
    b. More sunshine falls on Governors Island.
    c. Less sunshine falls on Manhattan Island.
    d. American cities should try to reduce the smoke.

3. I once read that the famous English art critic John Ruskin said he owed his fine sense of balance and form to the fact that as a child his only playthings were blocks. My own experience with children agrees with the conclusion of the experts that blocks are the one most important toy for both boys and girls. Long ago, I used to say that if my children could have only one plaything, it would be a nest of blocks.

Which statement comprises the main idea?

    a. John Ruskin had no playthings when he was a child.

    b. John Ruskin was a famous art critic.

    c. Children should have many toys.

    d. Blocks are the most important toys for children.

The answers are: 1-*c*; 2-*d*; 3-*d*.

It is a little difficult to determine the main idea because in each case the main idea is not specifically stated but must be inferred. Often writers of technical material will state their main idea in the first sentence and in these paragraphs all other statements will relate to that sentence. Whether it is easy or difficult to find the main idea, just keep your mind fixed on trying to find it, for in doing so you will improve your memory and your ability to concentrate.

The Chapter

Like the paragraph, the chapter also has structure and organization. Whenever you read, don't fail to notice how the author has organized the material and how each thought has a direct relationship to the whole theme. Should your concentration wane, or should you feel you are not quite understanding what you are reading, stop and reflect for a moment. Review the headings and subheadings, and you will soon reestablish yourself in comprehending what the author is saying. Sometimes it helps to first skim an article, just to get the general idea, and then read it more carefully.

The following selection is from the beginning of a chapter called "Life in the Antebellum Period." The title, together with the subhead ("Nationalism Unlimited") and the sidehead ("Confident America"), will give you an idea of how the material in the chapter is organized. This organization makes it easy to understand how nationalism was the expression of the increased confidence the American people had in the growth and prosperity of the country.

Chapter Thirteen

LIFE IN THE ANTEBELLUM PERIOD

"... the genius of the United States is not best or most in its executives or legislatures, ... but always most in the common people."

—WALT WHITMAN, 1855

1. Nationalism Unlimited

Confident America. To most Americans in the early 1850's it was wonderful just to be alive. The recent heated debate over the Wilmot Proviso had, it is true, raised dark warnings of disruption of the Union and even war. But in the compromise measures of 1850 good sense and devotion to the Union had once again prevailed over sectionalism, just as they had triumphed during the crises over Misssouri in 1819-1820 and Nullification in 1832-1833. Everywhere, in the South as much as in the North and West, men breathed loud sighs of relief when it seemed that all sections would accept the Compromise as the "final" settlement of the vexing issue of slavery in the territories. This was true especially after a hot fight over the Compromise in Georgia in 1851 resulted in a sweeping victory by the champions of the Union.

Of course there were dark clouds gathering just below the horizon. As we will soon see, Northerners were unwilling to accept one part of the Compromise, the Fugitive Slave Act. Southerners would not remain content with exclusion of slavery from any part of the territories. And pent-up tensions would erupt in secession and war at the beginning of the sixties. But this future was only dimly seen in the period before the war *(antebellum)*.

The fifties were a decade of high and generally sustained prosperity, except for a setback in 1857. Gold from California swelled the money supply. The frontier was expanding at a rapid pace. Foreign trade was growing by leaps and bounds. To a people who had just carved out a western empire, fulfilled their "Manifest Destiny," and were busy growing great, no problem seemed too difficult to solve.

Expanding national pride and jaunty confidence were evident on all sides throughout the fifties, even during the middle and latter years of the decade, when sectional strife once again was menacing. Aggressive nationalism permeated the popular literature and the speeches of politicians. It took form especially in the new twist that public spokesmen in the late 1840's and the 1850's gave to the older doctrine of "Manifest Destiny." Before about 1848 Americans had conceived of their destiny in terms of expansion to the Pacific Coast. Now they were beginning to think in bolder terms — of a mission to show the world, particularly decadent Europe, the superiority of democratic institutions; of a destiny, perhaps, to govern the entire Western Hemisphere!

To obtain a good idea of how to go about finding organized thoughts in material without subtitles, suppose you were to read an article entitled "Supreme Court Should Be Radically Changed." One way to approach this article would be to imagine that you are giving a speech. The first statement you would make is that the Supreme Court should be radically changed, and then you would give your reasons for saying this. After that, do you think you would describe *how* the Supreme Court should be changed? Of course you would. A great many speeches and articles follow just this simple logical organization, by relating to such questions as "what" (is it used for), "who" (does it apply to), "where," and "when."

Reducing Interference While Reading

Unless material is well organized, you may find yourself reading unrelated facts that hinder understanding and retard recall. Lack of organization can cause interference. You can make up for this by being careful to organize your own thoughts while reading. One way to do this is to make sure that you recognize patterns and classifications in what you are reading and that your thoughts relate to them. When well organized, a long chapter can be easier to commit to memory than a short one.

Discriminating While Reading

Ideas vary greatly in value. Statements may take up the same space on paper, but they must not take up equal space in your mind. Some statements should be skimmed, others should be read carefully, and still others should be reviewed and committed to memory.

Many of us do not discriminate while reading, which may be because of improper reading habits acquired in childhood. To overcome lack of discrimination, train yourself to recognize the difference between essential and less essential ideas as they relate to the main idea. Skimming a passage before carefully reading it can help you to do this.

One of the best ways to learn how to discriminate is to imagine yourself repeating the contents of an article or chapter to someone else. You wouldn't attempt to repeat it word for word, but would give a brief synopsis in your own words. As you imagine yourself giving this information to someone else, also try to visualize that person.

Having a Purpose While Reading

You can acquire, develop, and retain a sense of discrimination by trying to read with a purpose in mind. Concentration does not necessarily mean keeping the mind fixed on one object, or in one place. More accurately, when reading, it means keeping your thoughts moving toward a definite goal. Note that when your purpose is clearly defined, you can cruise through material at a very rapid rate and your mind will not wander. If you are looking up a name in the phone book, your eyes can run down the page at a remarkable rate; or if you are looking in an encyclopedia for some particular information — a famous person's birth date, for example — you can proceed quite rapidly until you come to such key words as born, or birth, or the date itself. Can you recall even one instance when your mind wandered at such a time?

Reading with the author's organization in mind and with the intention of absorbing his ideas, naturally assumes the act of reading with a purpose. Even if you are interested in other ideas or facts, your mind will nevertheless be open and receptive.

Establishing a Purpose While Reading

A good way to establish a purpose in reading is to ask questions. Let's say you want to read a technical article called "Functions of Living Cells." First you look at the title, then you look at the length of the article, then you look at its overall structure, and then you are ready to ask this question: Wouldn't it be better to have the title itself in question form, "What Are the Functions of Living Cells?" In doing this you can often clarify your purpose in reading, and thus be able to establish a purpose. When you are reading with a purpose, *you* are in command, because you are giving your entire attention to what you are doing.

Scanning and reading with a purpose are new habits to most people, and self-discipline is necessary. The small investment in time that it takes to scan and set a purpose will increase your reading ability and reduce mind wandering.

Let's not forget about the principle of finding a use, mentioned in Chapter 2. That concept and the concept of having a purpose while reading are not in conflict. In having a purpose while reading, you are looking for information that is in the material. In finding a use, you are being creative — you are thinking of ways to use the information in a real-life situation.

Let us take the following selection, "The Training of the Mind." What are some purposes that come to your mind just by noting the title? Think for a moment.

Perhaps you would like to find out how to train the mind. In other words, what must be developed in order to have a well-trained mind? Next your purpose might be to find out how each mental area can be developed. Okay, now read solely for those purposes. When you finish, it is your objective to look up and state what a well-trained mind consists of and how it can be developed. Afterwards, there will be five questions. You may note that you may read more rapidly than normal, yet you will be able to answer the questions despite the fact that the questions may not relate directly to your purposes. That is because you will be concentrating better.

One reminder before proceeding. The correct procedure is keeping purposes in mind *while reading*. You don't get to the end and then look back to find answers to your questions. You should feel the purposes being met as you read along.

THE TRAINING OF THE MIND

An important factor in the development of the mind is learning to pay attention. We can pay very close attention to a single thing for only a few moments at a time. An object must be constantly changing for us to notice it continuously. It is probable, too, that concentrated attention can be given to only one thing at a time. In considering two or more things at once, the mind shifts from one to the other. The range of our attention is really very limited and is likely to take in only general impressions. This is beneficial in some ways, for it is not always desirable to examine everything in detail. Many people, however, acquire the habit of paying only superficial attention to nearly everything; the mind "skims but never alights." We should train ourselves to be keen and rapid observers and yet be able to give close attention to one line of thought whenever necessary. Some things should be read rapidly; others studied closely.

How may we remember those things that are really worth keeping in mind? When we are able to remember ideas voluntarily as facts needed for some definite purpose, we consider them as having been learned. In learning something of importance it is advisable to impress it on the mind as deeply as possible, to repeat or recall it over and over again and to associate it closely with other facts already well established in the mind. The ability to remember is one of our most desirable possessions, especially in youth when the mind is so easily impressed.

Hence this ability should never be injured by neglect but instead, should be improved by training.

One of the chief purposes of going to school is to form good habits. Habits are great savers of time and mental energy. If it were not for them, we should have to be making up our minds concerning every small detail of our conduct, no matter how often we had made the same decision before. One of the principal concerns of the student, therefore, may well be to acquire helpful habits of mind through close attention and constant practice.

The ability to reason successfully is the crowning achievement of a trained mind. The first qualification that a good reasoner must have is a good stock of experience, for one can not reason well concerning things of which he knows little. Fortunately, he can greatly extend his experience by reading and study, thus taking the experiences of others as his own. Then he must have good judgment and finally he must also have a genuine desire to know the truth. This means that he must be willing to modify his previous ideas in the light of new understanding. Particularly, he must not consider a thing necessarily true because it has been believed for a long time or is believed by many people. He should weigh the evidence on any new and partially confirmed theories. He must not accept too many statements merely on the authority of someone else; yet he must sincerely try to understand the reasoning of those who have given the most thought to the problem. Only in this way can the reasoning power of the mind be efficiently trained.

Questions

1. Does constant change help or hinder us in giving attention to an object?
2. On how many objects at a time can one's attention be closely centered?
3. What is meant by a "superficial reader"?
4. What practical use of attention is mentioned by the writer?
5. When may we consider something as having been learned?

Cultivating Comparisons

When reading, try to find how one subject and method of presentation compares with another, and notice the similarities and differences. This will enable you to evaluate the advantages and disadvantages of the comparisons you have made.

In studying economics, for example, you might compare socialism with communism, and then the two with capitalism. You might find it convenient to discuss categories, such as how each of these systems deals with private property, with small businesses, with monetary matters, with work incentives, etc.

You should have a good idea of what constitutes a well-trained mind and how it can be developed if you set your purposes clearly. I should also mention that when reading you do not always need a well-organized sequence of ideas. The author may digress, but if *your* purposes are well established, you will read effectively.

Acquiring and Applying a Reading Technique

Okay. It's fine to look for organization and to discriminate, but how can organization and discrimination be applied in actual reading? You can apply them and the principles that follow by using a very simple technique. You should formulate a summary of the contents as soon as possible. Sometimes you can start your recall pattern even before reading, and then you can read for the purpose of finding those ideas that fit into your recall pattern.

We will illustrate this by returning to the Nationalism selection on page 47. The first two sentences can be formulated by just reading the chapter title and the main heading. Say to yourself: " 'Life in the Antebellum Period' was characterized by 'Nationalism Unlimited.' Nationalism came about because there was an increase in confidence during that period."

Notice how you already have a major portion of the summary. Now as to the next sentence, what do you think it should be? Shouldn't you ask at this point: "*Why* did confidence increase?" Of course! Underneath the heading "Confident America" there are four paragraphs. Since you know that each paragraph deals with one idea, is it not reasonable to assume that four reasons will be given for the growth of confidence? Yes, that is a reasonable assumption. However, the author actually only gives three reasons. One paragraph adds interest and perspective to the selection but not information. If you were reading for the purpose of gathering facts efficiently, you would not spend time on a paragraph once you see that it does not help your structure. The following technique helps you eliminate a paragraph quickly if it does not fit into your organized structure.

Now you are ready to read the entire selection. Your next thought will be "Confidence increased because ..." and then you read solely for the purpose of finishing the thought, noting the three points as you go along. When you organize your mind in accordance with what you are reading, you are using many of the principles discussed in Chapter 2. You are absorbing ideas in an organized manner and you will therefore be likely to recall in an organized manner. This is how learning and memory are enhanced simultaneously.

Another aspect of reading is that you are naturally forced to exercise discrimination. Knowing the date of the Compromise of 1850 and its attendant details will not help you to understand and remember why confidence increased. The most common cause of mind wandering is the reader's failure to realize that information differs in importance. Even if you need to recall *all* the details from something you are reading, it is best to first note the main ideas — you can always reread to refresh your memory on the less important ideas.

Setting Learning Goals in Reading

We have discussed how the importance of setting goals relates to numerous areas of self-improvement. Perhaps the most helpful suggestion we can make with respect to reading with a goal is that it is not necessary for you to count pages as part of that goal. In a quantitatively large assignment, you can divide the reading material into smaller units, by reading a few pages in a given period of time. In this way you can allow yourself a number of goals, made up of chapter headings, sub-headings, and so on. The smaller the unit of information the brain deals with, the more effective retention will be.

Creating an Experience

While things are happening all the time, not all happenings are experiences. Only when something affects you personally does a happening become an experience. Your mind has a natural tendency to focus on personal matters — otherwise, you become bored and easily distracted. It follows that one sure way to become involved while reading is to make it a personal experience. In reading history, try to identify with the customs, institutions, and people who were part of that history. As you read about Napoleon or Lincoln or Churchill, imagine yourself dealing with and solving the problems they faced. And as an American, when studying economics, you can certainly take a personal interest in the problems that a president faces which can affect the whole country.

Using All Your Mental Faculties to Concentrate

It is almost frightening to consider how little control we have over our conscious minds. If we tell ourselves to go to sleep because we must awaken early, it becomes ever so much more difficult to fall asleep. If we tell ourselves to remember an important date or name, we are no more likely to remember it than if we had not done so. If we pound the desk and tell ourselves to concentrate, we will very likely be unable to concentrate.

Consequently, it's necessary to muster all your mental powers and direct them toward absorbing material effectively. You cannot do this by force. Rather you must woo your mental powers to do your bidding. You can best do this by involving as many of your mental faculties as are within your power. In acquiring information you will encounter many opportunities to increase your visual imagery ability. The more you visualize while reading, the more you will be able to engage the visual area of your brain and thus enhance your ability to concentrate and to develop your memory.

Making the Best Use of a Photographic Memory

Some people speak of a photographic memory wistfully and assume that it means the ability to reproduce, in picture form, every detail that the eye sees or reads. There really is no such phenomenon as an *overall* photographic memory. No one can reproduce an entire page of reading matter from memory. Many people who claim to have a photographic memory have been questioned, and it was discovered that very few possess this faculty as a whole. Invariably, what they saw or read was enlarged or distorted by imagination; and in many instances, they omitted important details and remembered unimportant ones.

Nevertheless, there are people whose photographic, or visual memory is unusual. The real difference between them and those whose visual ability is not as well developed is that the former can visualize or picture a written word or scene, while the latter are more likely to recall the idea and meaning.

Generating Your Own Thoughts

Probably the surest way to have all your mental areas working in unison is to generate your own thoughts after reading. Thinking is "inner communication." Suppose you are about to start reading a difficult chapter on meteorology that deals with the causes of thunderstorms. First, you will recall all you know about water. Then you will recall something about clouds, winds, and electricity, about which you already have some knowledge. Finally, you'll try to think about and solve some of the problems that relate to thunderstorms. It is amazing how much you can accomplish by thinking logically.

All creative thinking is centered around a hypothesis. A hypothesis is a belief as to how matters will turn out, given certain conditions; and it is based on an underlying theory or understanding of a subject. From your own perhaps limited understanding of a subject, you can form your own hypothesis and say what you *think* the material is about. Then you can test your hypothesis by reading the material and by comparing your hypothesis with your understanding of what you have read. Most often your hypothesis will not be entirely correct on first reading. But on rereading, you will find that your hypothesis is closer to the actual meaning of the material than you expected.

There is a large speed-reading company that gives a demonstration which features a person who is a super-speed reader. This super-speed reader turns a page every eight seconds or so. When ten pages have been read, the super-speed reader looks up and astounds the audience by summarizing the contents of the material. Actually, this was not reading. No one can see each and every word at more than 1,600 words a minute. The super-speed reader was *scanning* — picking up key words and then putting them all together. This takes a certain amount of ability, considerable practice and a lot of courage.

Scanning should not be called reading because in scanning you do not see all the words. Nevertheless, it is an excellent skill to develop. You can try scanning yourself — perhaps not at 5,000 words per minute, but certainly between 1,000 and 2,000 words, which is within the range of the average individual. Do the scanning as quickly as possible and then, from your own knowledge, state what you believe the author has said. On rereading, you will find that you have been correct, surprisingly. Scanning will enable you to spend much less time reading and enable you to remember more. That's right. You will remember more because you yourself are actually involved in the reading. You have generated your own thoughts — which you will be more likely to remember than the thoughts of someone else.

Try the following passage. Scan it by reading only the first and last sentences of each paragraph. Then look up and think of a hypothesis relating to the author's intent. You may take a quick second look if you are not quite ready at the first reading. After you have clarified your hypothesis, read very rapidly to see if you were right. Your overall efficiency in terms of concentration and retention will be enhanced. Test yourself by answering the questions.

DIFFERENT KINDS OF COURAGE

Among uncivilized peoples, physical courage is one of the most essential of virtues. Not all primitive tribes are warlike, but many of them are, and even among the most peaceful there are many dangers to be met and overcome. There is danger from wild animals, from the elements, from hostile tribes, from the strong men of the tribe. The timid soul who lives in such an environment must be in never-ending mental distress. The brave are happier and more likely to survive. It is natural, then, that during the earlier years of human history it came about that physical bravery was extolled as a most praiseworthy characteristic, and cowardice was regarded as disgraceful. Once such conceptions find a place in the thinking of people, they are likely to be held for generations and centuries. They remain the accepted standards long after the conditions which gave rise to them have ceased to exist.

It is not to be assumed that such bravery is no longer useful. Physical courage still has its place in the world. It is especially serviceable to children, for they live in a world of dangers, or hurts and bruises, of quarreling and fighting, and the child who is too fearful of pain, too frightened at the prospect of a combat, will experience anxieties which may leave a permanent mark on the personality. In adult life, however, there is not the need there once was for bravery. Most men are relatively free from attack or threat of attack. The dangers which surround them, such as dangers of traffic, call for prudence and restraint rather than physical courage. A physical coward can get along better today than in earlier years. Courage, in the physical sense, is not the outstanding virtue it once was. Cowardice is not so great a handicap.

While, however, physical courage is coming to occupy a place of diminishing importance in modern life, the need becomes more compelling for intellectual and moral courage. To a greater extent than formerly we deal with ideas. We do not combat physical dangers so much but we need to have information and sound opinions about abstract matters. We need clear thinking. The penalty for failure to find out the truth is heavy. When, therefore, we allow ourselves to be deceived, when we fail to look facts in the face and to recognize them as such, even though they are unpleasant, when, in short, we lack intellectual courage, we suffer for it. And we suffer when we have not the moral courage to stand by our convictions, when we support a cause in which we do not believe, when we allow desire for gain or any other consideration to prevent us from doing what we believe to be right. Intellectual and moral courage are more essential virtues today than physical bravery, and one who is lacking in them is guilty of the worst kind of cowardice.

Questions

1. What is the most important characteristic among uncivilized peoples?

2. According to the writer, how was cowardice regarded in early times?

3. To whom is physical courage still especially valuable and useful?

4. What important cause of physical dangers in present-day life is mentioned by the writer?

5. What two characteristics are more valuable than bravery in meeting such a danger?

Thoughts are generated through reading critically. This matter of concepts and thoughts will be dealt with in the section on listening. We will simply say here that if you can develop a critical faculty, you can get more out of your reading.

Putting Key Words in Writing

Having read the preceding selection and having answered the questions, can you recall what each paragraph was about? Certainly, this would be rather difficult. But suppose you were given some key words, such as *attack*, *coward*, and *bravery*, would you then be able to recall each paragraph?

In recalling, other ideas and facts will come to mind. We can see how the reconstruction principle works to recall reading matter. Not only does a main idea recall supporting ones, but one key word can start the ball rolling. Is it true, then, that in order for you to learn how to remember any sequence of ideas all you have to do is to remember a list of key words? Yes, that is true.

It would therefore be helpful if you wrote down a few key words or phrases from whatever you are reading. The key word might relate to the subject, or a topic, or to the action part of the main idea. These words or phrases will help you in remembering and recalling.

There is an even better reason for writing down words. Just the act of holding a pen improves concentration. A pen tends to focus thoughts. When you hold a pen (or pencil), you are bringing the visual area forward. You are also using the motor area, because you are engaging in a body action. By these means all your mental faculties are engaged. It is well worth your time to take down just a word or phrase from each idea that you deem worthy of retention.

Associating Key Ideas

If you have organized the information, selected key ideas, and utilized as many of your mental resources as possible, you will have very little difficulty with a short-answer or multiple-choice test. Problems in recall occur when we have to communicate information to others. If you were the world's most knowledgeable person and were unable to use your knowledge to help others, you might as well be ignorant. There would be little gained by reading, or travel, or experience in general if what you knew could not be recalled and communicated to others.

Here is a typical problem in recall. You have read an interesting article and you are telling someone about it. "Really, what did the article say?" is the response. You are stopped by this seemingly thoughtless question. You may recall a minor point or two, and so you say, "Well, ask me a question." "But how can I ask a question if I don't know what the article is about?" is the proper answer. Or let's say that after you have finished a written examination you feel you have left out a large and necessary item of information. The following suggestions will help you avoid a similar situation in the future. First, write down the key words you wish to recall. They will serve to remind you of other words. Next, associate the key words in proper sequence, through some mnemonic device. You can do this by selecting some words or phrases from each key idea and putting them together to make a story.

Let's look again at "Life in the Antebellum Period" and its subheading "Nationalism Unlimited." Having evaluated the organization, we can see that of the three paragraphs under the heading "Confident America," each contains an idea about "Nationalism." Suppose you choose a cue for "Nationalism" — an American flag. By this means you would be placing yourself in the story in accordance with the principle of ego involvement.

Now picture yourself confidently holding an American flag and waving it at a foreign boat in the distance. Later, when someone mentions the word *nationalism*, you will see yourself holding the flag and waving it, and you will recall the headings "Nationalism Unlimited" and "Confident America," and continue the chain by remembering other parts of the selection.

Let's read the following selection, "What Went Wrong?" for recall, and let's do it with the idea in mind that we may want to deliver a talk on it. Your first step will be to select the key word for each of the five "mistakes." After reading the entire article you will find that these words can help you recall all the essential points. You can now chain these words together and test yourself later.

WHAT WENT WRONG?

Mobil believes the nation's energy goal can be simply stated: In the coming decade, to produce a larger proportion of the energy we use; in the longer term, to achieve a reasonable energy surplus. Since nobody can forecast exactly how much energy the U. S. will need, it will be prudent to end up with too much rather than not enough.

But before we talk about surpluses, or even improved self-sufficiency, we have to ask: Why the present crisis? What went wrong?

The questions are necessary, because a nation should be able to learn from its past mistakes.

• *Mistake # 1* is 20 years old. In 1954 the U.S. imposed price controls on natural gas shipped across state lines. In its eagerness to protect the consumer, the government focused on low prices for the short term. It gave short shrift to the consumer's long-term stake in security and adequacy of supply. The artificially depressed price of natural gas has produced today's shortage of natural gas, by stimulating demand while reducing the incentive to look for new supplies. Even under the best conditions, this shortage will be with us for years, and it will probably get a good deal worse before it gets any better.

• *Mistake # 2* was the failure in past years to allow oil companies to press the search for oil and gas fully enough on the U. S. outer continental shelf. Reaction to the Santa Barbara spill caused too many people to lose their perspective. We must work to prevent spills and at the same time move ahead to try to assure adequate supplies.

Britain will be self-sufficient in oil about 1990, because it has actively promoted exploration under the seas around it, while the U. S. still puts "off limits" signs on thousands of square miles of outer continental shelf waters.

• *Mistake # 3* was the failure to permit construction of the Alaska pipeline to begin much earlier. The pipeline raised legitimate questions about the environment. But scare tactics led to overreaction. Result: the line — designed to safeguard both terrain and wildlife on the basis of probably the most detailed ecological analysis ever made — was unnecessarily stalled in the courts and in Congress when it should have been pumping oil into the American economy.

• *Mistake #4* was the nation's snail's-pace development of other energy sources. Construction of atomic power plants has been delayed for a variety of reasons. Coal — our country's most abundant energy source — was clobbered from all sides. It couldn't compete with the artificially low prices imposed on natural gas (which in turn held down the price of another competitor, home heating oil), nor could it compete with low-cost foreign oil in the Fifties and Sixties. Finally, a lot of coal was made unusable by tight limitations on sulfur content.

Ironically, too, the *expectation* of cheap atomic energy discouraged investments in new coal mines — so that the country got the worst of both worlds. There were and are legitimate environment concerns with both atomic energy and coal. But the nation has let itself be steered away from the basic question: "How much energy do we need, how soon, and at what economic and other cost?"

• *Mistake # 5* was the naive belief by many that we could rely indefinitely on getting all the foreign oil we wanted at the price we wanted to pay for it — so that we could continue to waste energy and avoid correcting mistakes # 1, 2, 3, and 4.

It could have been worse, of course. Remember the people who wanted to make the U. S. even more dependent on foreign oil, while assuring you that "national petroleum security" was a fiction devised by oil barons to keep domestic petroleum prices up? Remember the people who said not to worry about balance-of-payments problems, because these always righted themselves? And the instant tax experts eager to make sweeping changes, with little concern for the consequences? Fortunately, we didn't go all the way down any of those primrose paths.

Even so, for at least another 10 years, the U. S. is going to be heavily dependent on imported oil (coming increasingly from the Middle East), because of the long lead times that are unavoidable both in conserving energy on a large scale and in developing additional supplies.

To make a substantial reduction in energy use will require large investments by industry, new building standards for structures of all sorts, large numbers of low-horsepower cars replacing higher-horsepower cars year after year, the development of adequate public transportation systems, and other efforts.

It will take years, and very substantial investments, to discover and develop a new offshore oil field, or to get a new coal mine into operation or a nuclear power plant built.

Remember this when anyone tells you we can wait 10 years to even initiate any major effort.

Practicing a Recall Pattern

Read an article and try to formulate a recall pattern. In other words, consider how you would relay the information as quickly as possible. Then select the key words that relate to points supporting your pattern and tie them together with a visual chain of associations. Review the chain once and then try to recall it. You will be amazed at your ability. Continual practice will make you more skillful and effective.

Acquiring a Super-Memory

Thus far you have been shown how to associate relatively small items of information. But suppose you, a creative reader, think of applying the association principle to larger items — such as a full chapter, or even an entire book. Much depends on how general you wish to make your association. On the other hand, it is possible to memorize smaller ideas. With regard to the "Nationalism" selection, you could carry the process still further by associating the ideas in a paragraph with a word like *prosperity* — supported by facts such as gold being discovered in California. Under normal circumstances, however, it would not be worth the effort because it would be just as difficult to associate these relatively minor details as it would be to associate the major topics. Most likely, if you have read the material, all you need is to be reminded of the topic — the large chunk of information — and that will remind you of the supporting ideas and facts.

Are Visual Chains for You?

At this point you may be thinking that visual associations are good for those rare super-minds who can construct and remember easily — but that you are not one of those so gifted. Although people vary in their ability to create and visualize associations, the chances are that you possess more proficiency in these techniques than you realize.

I hope that you will remember to do more about mnemonics and visual chains than simply nod in agreement. They can be very useful to you.

Letter Association

One of the most effective methods of association is to use the initial letters of words. Suppose we want to remember the first three principles in Chapter 2. We could use the letters *O S D* and form the phrase "Old Soldiers Die." *O* can stand for Organization, *S* can stand for Serial Reconstruction, and *D* can stand for Discrimination. The letters and the phrase do not have to make sense. If you review what each letter stands for by reciting the relationship a few times, the key ideas will be firmly embedded in your memory.

In some instances, letter associations require less work to commit to memory than chaining ideas into a story. Also, words or terms that cannot be visualized, such as *repression* and *comprehension,* are more readily adapted to letter association. However, it sometimes happens that cues (letters) are remembered while the words they stand for are not.

In general, the use of letter associations should depend on two considerations. First, the connection of the letter will retrive the key word. Second, thought should be given to the importance of remembering the key word itself. It is not as necessary to remember the word *confidence* as it is to remember the general concept. Other words indicating more or less the same thing can be used to convey the idea; therefore, a visual picture would be more suitable. On the other hand, many situations call for the use of the correct professional term. To try to write about *repression*, an abstract word, without being able to remember the exact word, would be awkward to say the least. In this case, letter associations would be favorable because they connect directly to the desired word.

Reviewing

A businessman once told me that he reads *The Wall Street Journal* on the train to work, and although he finds the articles interesting, he can never seem to remember what they were about. Naturally! Reading a number of unrelated articles in one sitting will cause considerable interference, which is compounded when the businessman gets to work. I suggested that he might remedy this by taking just a few moments, before he leaves the train, to review the main ideas of each article. Once material has been read, it would be foolish not to take the proper steps to retain it. Review takes far less time than actual reading.

Recoding

Recoding is really a form of reciting, using one's own words. As you progress to higher levels, the importance of recoding increases. Ideally, in liberal arts courses, recoding adds a measure of interpretation, by means of which opinions and attitudes are communicated as one's own. There is nothing wrong with interpreting some data subjectively as it relates to memory. Practically everything remembered is recoded in some degree.

Recoding is also summarizing. While reading, it is helpful to look up after a page or two and restate in your own words the gist of what you have been reading. The ability to put much thought into a few words is very useful. And for the understanding of highly complex material, recoding and repetition may be the only way to retain it and communicate it.

Imagine a Use

Let's imagine several situations where we can put to use the techniques we have discussed so far.

Visual associations should be used when you are preparing an essay test or a speech. You don't always know when the need to recall information will arise. How often have you left a meeting or ended a conversation that dealt with a subject you read about but were unable to contribute to it information you knew you had. In such a situation, you would not want to make elaborate visual associations but you would like to have some information at hand.

The following procedure should be used to prepare for such an eventuality. First, after finishing an article, imagine all the possible instances that would cause you to say something like, "Oh, I read an article on that subject recently — 'The End of the Baby Boom.' It says that fewer babies are being born in this decade than in the previous decade. A few reasons for this are given, and then it describes the effect of this situation on the nation's economy."

What use could you have for this information? Under what conditions might you need it? Could you think of of a meeting of a school board at which someone suggests purchasing land for a new school? Could you imagine what you would say at such a meeting?

Or perhaps you can think of an investors' meeting at which someone suggests investing in a company that manufactures toys. What would you say at such a meeting? Can you think of other situations in which you would be likely to remember the article you read? Try to visually construct each situation as clearly as possible. Mentally construct the meeting, the people, yourself — everything pertinent, in a three-dimensional image.

Finally, see yourself offering the information in a way that is convincing. If you implement what has been said here, any situation that even remotely resembles those we have mentioned here will serve to trigger your memory.

Summary

We can see that reading is a creative activity. It requires a plan of approach. Certainly, it would be impossible to apply all the reading techniques we have discussed to any one situation. The technique(s) you use will depend on the kind of demand made on your knowledge of the material you are reading, and also on the structure and level of its difficulty.

Yet whatever the nature of the material or the circumstances, you cannot let your brain remain passive and inactive, and just go on reading words.

When incoming information is handled properly, it is selected, organized, interpreted, understood, and related.

Chapter Four

MEMORIZING FACTS AND DETAILS

Committing facts to memory requires the application of three principles that we have discussed thus far: organization, discrimination, and visual association. With these principles in mind, let's look at some basic facts that relate to Plato's philosophy. Plato was very much concerned with different aspects, of society: education, the organization of society, and who shall rule the state.

You might, as a student, undertake to study separate aspects of Plato's philosophy: (1) *education* — to prepare every member of society for assuming his proper place in that society; (2) *organization of society* — to allow everyone to participate in a harmonious, moral, and just order; (3) *who should rule* — according to Plato, the rulers of the state should be composed of the wisest men.

You can make your task easier and at the same time strengthen and broaden your knowledge by undertaking similar organization for Aristotle and other philosophers. You may even organize your thoughts topically, that is, you may take the topic "who shall rule," for example, and first list what Plato said, then what Aristotle had to say, and so on.

Generally, all philosophers have a basic premise or an underlying assumption from which they develop their ideas regarding life and society. To organize your learning process and to remember what you have learned, it is necessary to find the basic premise of a philosopher, and then see how it relates to his other ideas.

Plato's basic premise was his belief in a world of ideals, where everything was perfect and unchanging. He pictured a world of truth, goodness, and beauty. In his view, complete knowledge was unattainable, but individuals differed in their capacity to acquire and appreciate knowledge.

Thus it was his thought that the state should strive to become as close as possible to the ideal and to be so organized that all its citizens would be able to enjoy a just and harmonious life. He felt that the aim of education should be to bring out the inherent wisdom each person possesses, so that each would be equipped to participate in the society of which he or she is a part. The ruling class, according to Plato, should be made up of those who have the most wisdom and the most knowledge of what is good, true, and just. The judgment of those so endowed should be based on ideals and ideas rather than on the selfish, common instincts of untrained masses.

From the above we can see the facts of Plato's philosophy as they relate to his major premise. We can see a meaning and logic in it. We are not acquiring isolated facts that do not relate to his basic philosophy. By studying and learning what Plato and Aristotle and other philosophers have to say, we acquire knowledge without too much effort. We may not always be able to remember every one of their ideas on education, for instance, but we will certainly find it easier if we have a grasp of their basic principles.

Locating the Subject

Test yourself on your ability to recognize the subject or topic of a paragraph. What is the following paragraph about?

Hemoglobin is found in the red blood cells. It is a remarkable substance which is able to combine loosely with oxygen where oxygen is plentiful as in the lungs, and to release oxygen where it is less plentiful.

The subject of this paragraph is

a. Red blood cells.
b. Oxygen.
c. Hemoglobin.

Hopefully, you answered *c.* It may be that red blood cells contain hemoglobin, but this particular paragraph is about hemoglobin and not about red blood cells. The only basis you could have for giving oxygen as the answer is that it is mentioned often.

Locating the Details

As we said in our discussion on discrimination, ideas vary in value and in the way they should be treated. Some statements should be glossed over, others read carefully, and still others may be important enough to associate. In the following paragraphs, the subject is given in italics. Your object is to pick out the most important statement from the choices offered. In other words, pick out the idea that you would use to associate with the subject (Ivan IV is the subject for number 1).

1. *Ivan IV*

In 1547 Ivan crowned himself czar. Under his reign the brutal security police flourished.

    a. In 1547 Ivan crowned himself czar.

    b. Under his reign, the security police flourished.

2. *American Schools, 1870 to 1900*

In 1870, about seven million children were enrolled in American schools. By the turn of the century, that figure more than doubled. Also, during this same period, the number of high schools multiplied tenfold. The Industrial Revolution drastically changed the character of American schools.

    a. In 1870, about seven million children were enrolled in American schools.

    b. The number of high schools multiplied tenfold during this period.

    c. The Industrial Revolution drastically changed the character of American schools.

3. *Eisenhower Doctrine*

In January 1957, President Eisenhower asked Congress to authorize him to use military force if such was requested by any Middle Eastern nation and to set aside a sum of $200,000,000. Congress granted both requests.

    a. The Eisenhower Doctrine requested a sum of $200,000,000, which was granted.

    b. It authorized use of military force to protect the Middle East nations.

    c. It happened in January 1957.

4. *Adam Smith*

Shortly after his book *The Wealth of Nations* was published, Adam Smith was hailed as the father of political economy. He urged the government not to interfere with private business and advocated free trade between nations.

    a. He urged free trade and noninterference by government.

    b. He was hailed as the father of political economy.

The correct answers are:

    1*b*. What a person did, how that person affected history, is normally more important than when he did it or anything else about the person.

    2*c*. All the statements support and lead up to the last which should be associated first.

    3*b*. Naturally you must first know what the Eisenhower Doctrine was for before you can go on to anything else.

    4*a*. When studying about a person, it is usually of first importance to know what the person believed or stood for and his reasons for believing as he did. Anything else is relatively minor.

In each of these paragraphs, the correct procedure is to associate the main idea first, regardless of its order of appearance in the paragraph. Remembering the main ideas often serves to recall those of lesser importance. If for one reason or another you feel that the other statements or facts are also important, you should then associate the other facts in a visual chain. The chain should start with the object, subject, or person studied. The subject should then be associated first with the most important idea. Therefore, the procedure entails three steps in sequence.

1. Locate the subject of the paragraph or group of facts.
2. Find the facts or details that you decide are important or should be remembered.
3. Associate the subject with the important facts, preferably using a visual chain.

The third step is to use artificial associations combining the subject with the desired details. We form a visual chain, starting with the subject, and then connect all other desired facts.

We can illustrate this procedure by referring to the passage on hemoglobin. Our objective is to arrange our memories in such a manner that when we are asked about hemoglobin, certain facts will come to mind. First we select a visual cue for the subject, hemoglobin. Let us use "globe." Anything associated with "globe" will tell us something about hemoglobin. We now form a chain of visual cues. Picture the globe floating in a giant red blood cell. Recalling this vision will tell us where hemoglobin is found. The cell floats past a cluster of oxen (cue for oxygen) and the oxen are drawn to the globe. As the cell travels along sparser area, the oxen are distributed. Ludicrous though this may seem, key concepts such as where hemoglobin is found and that it combines with and releases oxygen will not be forgotten once you recall the globe and its associates.

At this point we must note that since we all think differently, our choice of cues and associations will be different. This is fine as long as our associations are clear and visual and include all the necessary facts.

Any fact or group of facts can be committed to memory through association. If a drug salesman wants to remember all the items in his line of products, he might associate this way. Let's say he wants to remember Empirin. It contains caffeine and aspirin. So, he pictures himself standing next to the Empire State Building (cue for Empirin) while drinking coffee, which makes him wide awake (cue for caffeine), and so he takes an aspirin. Later, when asked the ingredients in Empirin, he is able to recall them by picturing the Empire State Building.

Classification and Association Work Together

Very often you can associate a fact with a situation rather than with a name, place, object, or idea, as in this example: An advertising marketing manager deals with dozens of accounts, each with its own advertising manager, product manager, sales promotion manager, artist, and copywriter. And the marketing manager has to deal with all of these people. He is constantly confusing the advertising manager of Avon with the sales promotion manager of Johnson & Johnson and both of them with the product manager of Bendix. He keeps very neat notes, but sometimes this proves to be time-consuming and embarrassing.

The author showed the marketing manager how, if he is confusing the product manager at Bendix, for example, with someone else, he can immediately draw on his extensive mental file, consisting of people, positions, and companies, and come up with the right name.

His first step will be to organize his material properly. Instead of aimlessly trying to remember a name, position, and company, he can start with the company and commit each position in the company to memory in a set order. First, he will remember the advertising manager, then the sales promotion manager, then the product manager, then the copywriter, and last the artist. (The reason for this particular order will be explained later.) He puts each company in a separate category, and that decision alone can aid his memory.

The next step is to select cues for each company and associate each person's name in the order designated by his or her position in the company. Take the first company, Pepsi Cola, and visualize a bottle of Pepsi. Let's say the advertising managers name is Baron (Pepsi is being drunk by a baron). The sales promotion manager is Parkinson (drinking Pepsi takes place in a park). The product manager is Wendt and he thinks of "windy" if he has had any dealings with the man. The copywriter is Manchester (the wind blows against the baron's chest.)

And the artist is Crowley (somehow, place a crow in the story). Suppose you review this chain, but bear in mind that you can always choose your own associations.

The next step is not really a step but evidence of the fact that you do not have to remember each person with the job title. All you have to do is remember the name and note the position along the chain, and you will have the job title. To review, if you want to know the **product manager** of Pepsi Cola, you visualize the Pepsi bottle, see the visions being recalled, and note that wind is the third association. You would then know that the name that reminds you of wind is the product manager of Pepsi. Why? Because you kept the same order of job titles for all the companies. The product manager is always the third association.

The last step is not really necessary if you are actually using a system like the one described. Nevertheless, at the beginning, it may be necessary to establish an aid in order to remember the sequence of the job titles. A cross association is also suggested, such as *A* for Advertising Manager, *S* for Sales Promotion Manager, *P* for Product Manager, and so on until the letter chain *ASPCA* is formed. Hence the reason for the particular order of job titles.

Now you can try a company on your own, using your own cues and story chain. Practice, concentrate, review, and then test your knowledge of Pepsi Cola and the other company, which is Avon. Select your cue for Avon. Here are the personnel:

Advertising Manager — Wolff

Sales Promotion Manager — Carvelli

Product Manager — Forrest

Copywriter — Burton

Artist — Chicorel

I hope you created a truly wild, no holds barred story. Now without looking back, see if you can answer these questions:

1. Who is the Sales Promotion Manager of Pepsi Cola?

2. Who is the Product Manager of Avon?

3. Who is the Advertising Manager of Pepsi?
4. Who is the artist of Avon?
5. What position does Wolff hold at Avon?
6. What position does Manchester hold at Pepsi?

If you committed the chains to memory and tested yourself, I'm sure you are aware of the enormous potential in using a system such as this. Doubtless you can see that with a slight variation this system could also have been used to remember the views of the philosophers.

The principle of association can be of great help to you. The real skill is in being creative, in finding ways of utilizing the techniques of association for your own requirements.

Memory Relating to Foreign and Technical Words

In Chapter 2 we briefly showed how association techniques can aid in the learning and recall of foreign words. And while association may not be as applicable in learning grammar and some of the finer points of a language, it can help in acquiring the basic vocabulary.

To study vocabulary, whether that of a foreign language or of a scientific or specialized field, such as chemistry or the law, it is best to learn the meaning and correct usage first, and then to associate. The principle of organization can also be helpful in acquiring a vocabulary.

Take the word *psychopathology: psycho, path,* and *ology* are root words meaning "mind," "disease," and "study," respectively. We can see why *psychopathology* means "the study of diseases of the mind."

Learning the derivation of a word will help you to realize that a word is not just assigned an arbitrary meaning. Knowing a derivation can give you an insight into structure as well as meaning. You will, in addition, strengthen your memory as you acquire a larger vocabulary. Learning new words will also give you a certain amount of satisfaction. Students often make the mistake of trying to figure out the meaning of a word without looking at it in relation to the sentence in which it occurs. It is therefore suggested that you read the sentence carefully and try to figure out the meaning of a word that is not clear to you by analyzing it in its context. Then you can check to see if you are correct. If you are, fine. If not, your overall concentration will be enhanced anyway because you have used the principle of ego involvement in learning and adding to your vocabulary.

Summary

Whenever you commit a fact to memory, you must connect a subject or topic with the information that relates to the fact. If you want to connect a name with a face, the face is the subject and the name constitutes the information. In the case of the meaning of a word, the word is the subject and the meaning is the information. In remembering the time and place of an event, the event is the subject and the time and place are the information.

The first step is to be sure of your subject or topic. Then select some aspect of that subject or topic that is easier to deal with. This may involve a prominent or unusual feature if you are remembering a face or location; or perhaps a more concrete or familiar word within a word if you are dealing with, for instance, a term in chemistry. In some instances you may select a key word or phrase. Whatever you select, you are now ready to use it and not worry about the larger unit for the time being.

From this point you will have just one item of information to connect to your subject or topic. However, if you have more than one item, you must organize your information. The most important item will usually go first, although you may occasionally have reason to remember a particular sequence without regard to importance, as in the advertising field example. Now select a cue (or cues) for the information, and then associate, preferably using visual imagery.

Finally, to recall, you would look at, think about, or visualize (whichever you choose) your subject and ask yourself what you picked out. This will come back to you, and you can then relate the cues to it.

Chapter Five

HOW TO LISTEN TO A LECTURE

The problem with concentrating *and* listening is that too many irrelevant thoughts enter the mind. If such thoughts could be screened out, concentration would be greatly enhanced. We have already noted that mind-wandering while reading is caused by feeding information to the brain at a rate that is boring. This problem of mind-wandering is even more prevalent in listening because our brains are capable of processing information at about four times the rate of speaking.

Furthermore, to add to the problem, many people speak slowly and with long pauses. Sometimes, several seconds may elapse between meaningful thoughts. When we must wait a few seconds between these thoughts we are, in effect, expecting our minds to go blank during that time. Very often, our minds will refuse to tolerate the strain and will wander.

What Not to Do

Many listeners will try to sustain attention by forcing themselves to repeat each word they hear. If concentration can be sustained in this way, the listener deserves a medal for determination. The mind works best, however, when it deals in thoughts and ideas — not in exact words. So the first thing to do is to stop wasting mental energy in trying to repeat word for word what the speaker is saying.

The Active Mind

The basic problem with concentrating while listening is that the mind has too much time to generate irrelevant thoughts. If, however, the intervening thoughts are directly related to what the speaker is saying, then concentration and memory will be improved. Remember, the more active a mind is, the more alert and receptive it will be to information. A thinking, busy mind does not tire, as does a muscle.

Interject Your Own Thoughts

It's too bad we can't press an "input" button in our brains and have information recorded. The world around us is constantly changing, and we must adjust to these changes. Consequently, the knowledge we possess is as much due to our own thoughts as it is to what the environment offers. Maximum learning takes place when the learner merges his own knowledge with information he is receiving.

Suppose a biology lecturer states that the nerves of the central nervous system (brain and spinal cord) do not regenerate if destroyed. You may recall a previous lesson in which you learned that the nerves of the peripheral nervous system (arms, legs, etc.) *can* regenerate. It then becomes clear to you why a spinal injury can be very serious indeed, often leading to paralysis. You will surely retain this insight because you yourself thought of it. You have contributed some prior knowledge to new information and this synthesis made you aware of a biological phenomenon.

Think of Examples

A more common method of acquiring knowledge from a lecture is to think of examples. If the speaker says, "The United Nations has settled many minor disputes between large nations and many major disputes between small nations . . . ," a number of examples supporting this statement can be cited by someone who is abreast of the subject.

Anticipate

The careful, well-informed listener can often anticipate what the speaker will say next. This anticipation involves personal concern with the subject and a certain amount of feeling. If you have anticipated correctly, you will have a feeling of satisfaction. Even if the speaker has not come up to your expectations, anticipation has made your mind all the more alert and attentive.

Ask Questions

Seeking answers to questions can help in organizing your thoughts and in keeping your mind receptive. As a rule, speakers don't mind being asked questions. Asking questions sometimes changes a lecture or a discussion from one that is purely academic and impersonal to one that is highly personal and emotionally stimulating. Having raised an issue and having received a direct answer makes for a stronger and more lasting impression of the experience. Afterwards, if you forget what the speaker said, you can start a chain of memories backward by first asking yourself whether you remember asking a question, and the answer that followed will come to you. This in turn will help to bring back a memory of still more that happened at the lecture.

Summarize

Even the most accomplished lecturer can sometimes stray from the main topic. You should therefore keep in mind the overall theme, purpose, or idea of the lecture. If you try to summarize from time to time while the lecture is going on, you will keep your mind occupied and strengthen your memory. Summarizing as the lecture proceeds can be done with speed. This ability to think at high speed will enable you to carry on the necessary mental activities as you follow the speaker.

Criticize

Develop the habit of using your critical faculties. This means linking what the speaker says with what you already know, and noting whether you agree or not with what you have heard. Lectures on the liberal arts, for example, often have a particular perspective or personal slant. Topics in the political and social sciences can often evoke conflicting responses. The alert listener will be able to identify and subvocalize his or her own reactions and feelings. Later, in recall, it is possible to start a chain of memories rolling back concerning whether or not you agreed with the lecturer.

Take Notes

By all means take notes if you feel insecure in relying solely on your memory. Note taking can even be helpful in learning, because it engages the motor areas of the brain thereby enhancing memory and concentration. You will find that the mind has less of a tendency to wander when taking notes.

One disadvantage may be that you are so busy trying to record every single word of the speaker, you are aware only of the words and not the thoughts. You can achieve a happy medium if while taking notes, you recognize the difference between main ideas and details.

Probably the best note-taking method is to draw a line down the center of your notebook page, and reserve the right side for main ideas and the left side for supporting ideas and details. This will make it necessary for you to exercise your judgment as to which is a main idea and which is a detail or subsidiary idea. It should also help you recognize statements that should not be taken down at all. The activity of making this mental judgment will also facilitate your rereading of your notes later.

Good Listening Requires Practice

Listening, anticipating, criticizing, summarizing, interjecting, thinking of examples, concentrating, asking questions, and writing — all require quite a bit of mental work. The result, however, is very much worth the effort.

Listening is nòt something that you can turn on once you learn the proper way to listen. It must be practiced. Just because you have been shown how to do a new dance step does not mean that you will execute it properly the first time. You must evoke a good visual picture of the step, and keep it in mind as you attempt it. The same is true of listening. You should sit down prepared to use all the methods of keeping your mind involved with the speaker in addition to taking notes. Very rarely will you be required to use all the techniques of listening at one lecture, but as long as you are prepared to listen, the greater will be your chances of recalling.

Summary

Thus far we have discussed several principles of concentration with regard to reading and listening. Don't think in terms of "this material is for reading and this is for listening" because there is no such sharp distinction. By definition, a principle is broad, flexible, and far-reaching. When reading, you should be concentrating and exercising your critical faculty so that you may interject your own thoughts in an organized and purposeful way. You will need to do the same when listening to a lecture, with the difference that you will have to listen more attentively. And whether reading or listening, your emotional and personal involvement are the same, and you need to apply the principles of concentration.

Chapter Six

WAYS AND MEANS OF STUDYING

In the ever-accelerating demands made on us today, it is clear that good study habits are an asset at any age. The methods and principles discussed in the section on reading can help you to become a good student.

Learning is a complex activity. Study requires skill. Assignments vary in length, difficulty, and depth of knowledge required. Students vary even more than their assignments. As to a plan of study, the following general practices can be adapted to your own needs: preparing, reading, memorizing, and reviewing.

Preparing

The object of preparing is to activate the neural cells and pathways so they will be ready to accept the forthcoming information. Retrieving all the prior information you possess on a certain subject accomplishes this.

Scanning

Scanning is the means by which you prepare your mind to accept what you are about to learn. There are a number of different ways to scan. One way is to force your eyes to travel down the page as rapidly as possible, picking out key words or terms. This method is particularly applicable where the material you are to study has no subtitles and is not too difficult. Another way to scan is to read the first and last lines of a paragraph, especially when the material has headlines, divisions, and subdivisions.

Very often the best way to begin scanning is to look for something that arouses your curiosity or interest. You'll have to be careful not to just keep on reading — or you'll get bogged down and forget that you are really studying.

If you find yourself interested, you won't regard studying as a task, and you will be aware of learning, both emotionally and intellectually.

Since you will be studying at your own pace, the amount of time you take will be your own decision. Sometimes, preparing yourself to study may take only a few minutes, sometimes it may take longer. There is nothing wrong with taking longer to prepare the mind to receive information. The investment in time is well worth the effort.

Reading

Don't overlook the questions that often appear at the end of study material. Try to answer them. They can be useful as a refresher, a basis for review, and an aid to memory. Besides, you can be sure that such questions have been very carefully chosen by the author and are suggested because they are worth your consideration. You should use any means — visual aids, pictures, summaries, or relevant materials — to strengthen your purpose in reading.

Finding Organization

Whether you are reading and studying in order to write an essay or prepare for a short-answer test or a quick quiz, you will have to do a certain amount of memorizing. Preparing for memorization means that you should note relationships of subtitles, establish associations, and use as many mnemonic techniques as necessary. Whether you study at a fast or slow pace, you still must do a certain amount of memorizing — it is a most valuable aspect of your study efforts.

Memorizing

Learning and memorizing are interrelated. Make sure that the key ideas are firmly fixed in your mind. They will be of inestimable help to you, whether you are going to take a short-answer test or are preparing for a writing assignment.

Reviewing

By the time you are ready to review what you have learned, you yourself will have become the best judge of how much you have understood and retained. Reciting, recording, and repeating are important elements in reviewing a subject. (You may want to reread the pertinent parts of Chapter 2 before you begin.) Generally, the broader your knowledge, the more time you should spend recoding rather than reviewing. Liberal arts subjects usually call for recoding, while technical and scientific subjects call for more recitation — both are intended to strengthen retention.

Reviewing for a Short-Answer Test

Studying with other students can be helpful to each of you. You can take turns asking questions and learn something at the same time. Short-answer tests in particular lend themselves to this method. When your turn comes to ask a question you can think of yourself as the teacher who has to evaluate the answers.

Self-Testing

Knowledge depends on the *depth* of your reading and study and what has been retained. It is therefore necessary to keep testing yourself. If you ask yourself questions about what you have read, you will often find that you do not have as clear a grasp of the material as you thought. Once you are aware of this, you can do something to correct it: recite to yourself, preferably aloud, as you go along.

When to Study

When you should study is up to you. Ideally, you should study many times during a semester and allow for frequent intervals of review. What you should study first is also up to you. Some people like to study the most difficult or the least interesting material first; others prefer to leave them for last. The order in which you study is not as important as the degree of concentration you bring to your studies and the amount of information you are able to retain. And there isn't anything wrong in concentrated study just before an exam, provided you can put in some solid, uninterrupted hours.

Preparing for Class

In most college courses, reading assignments are correlated with the lectures and the class discussions that follow. It is a good way of implementing a lecture, for very often a student comes to class unprepared and is hardly able to follow what is said. Although you should read your assignment beforehand and be prepared, it is not necessary to have mastered your assignment completely. You should be sure to know it enough to be able to listen and absorb the lecture intelligently.

As we learned in Chapter 2, comprehension depends to a large extent on the amount of related knowledge that you already possess. Unless you are interested in chemistry, for instance, you wouldn't get anything out of a technical talk on the subject. But a lecture on a subject you are familiar with can do wonders to increase your knowledge and help you in remembering.

Summary

Study is an activity in itself. You cannot approach a study assignment by casually starting with the first word, plodding through to the last word, and then closing the book. Study, to be rewarding, requires a plan of attack. There are a number of different ways to approach study, though to a certain extent what you do depends on the type of material you have to study and your general objective.

You will be a better student if you learn to use the techniques mentioned in this chapter and elsewhere in this book, particularly those relating to reading, listening, and remembering. A reminder: the principle of goal setting should be adhered to. Have clearly in mind your short-range goals, your medium-range and goals, and your long-range goals.

Chapter Seven

WAYS AND MEANS OF REMEMBERING
IN SPECIFIC AREAS

Remembering and Delivering a Speech

Remembering a speech does not mean remembering every word. It means remembering thoughts and ideas and points and conclusions. This will be easier to do if your speech is well written. Plan you speech so that everything in it is arranged in a logical sequence. Your audience will respond better to your speech and remember more of it if you do.

In writing a speech it is also necessary to recognize that some things are more important than others. You should try to develop a sense of discrimination.

Once you are satisfied that your speech is well organized, you are ready to voice what you have written. Taping your speech and listening to the playback can be very helpful when you are practicing. When delivering your actual speech, try to rely on your memory rather than on notes. If you prefer to use notes, however, you can do so in a way that is hardly noticeable.

To avoid the nervousness or distraction that may overwhelm you at the time you make the speech, it is a good idea to establish a visual chain and a letter chain, or a combination of both. You can make a list of the main ideas of your speech, take cues or key words from the list, and chain them together. Then you can establish an association of these main points, and in delivering the speech, have them clearly in mind.

It would be foolish to construct a chain with a cue for every sentence. A simple chain is best. It will make it easier to remember key points and can help you to avoid getting tongue-tied or suffer a loss of memory.

Letter associations are especially useful. A good speaker will generally need only a hint of a letter to remind him of a main idea. This main idea will evoke other ideas or examples and thus avoid a mental block because of nervousness.

Let's review the procedure. First, make a list of the key words or points. Then select a word or phrase from each of them. Then select a letter from each word or phrase — a letter that is the beginning of a key word, and that should serve as a cue. Chain these together, not as a word that necessarily makes sense but as a memory nudge.

To assure retention, visualize the word in your mind. As we said earlier, visualize in vivid colors and in three dimensions.

A final word. While speaking, keep your mind active. Keep thinking ahead to the next point or to the next association. Don't let yourself be mesmerized by the sound of your own voice.

Remembering in a Debate

The ability to engage in a debate requires knowledge, experience, and a good memory. Here we will deal only with that aspect of a debate that involves memory.

In a debate you adopt a point of view that is opposite to that of your opponent. To defend your point of view you reach into the storehouse of your memory for facts, arguments, and examples, and present them to your opponent. It is not uncommon for a person who has engaged in a debate to undergo self-criticism afterward because some particular point was overlooked.

The problem is mainly one of recall. You must have the ability to marshal your information in the correct order. Here are some suggestions. Prepare yourself to recall, try to anticipate the arguments of your opponent, and rehearse answers to them, point for point. Once the debate has started, your mind must be active until the end. As you listen to your opponent's presentation, think of ways to counter it. Always have a pencil and pad handy to make notes. If the debate brings out too much emotion, try to "cool it" by assuming an analytical, impersonal approach to your opponent and to his or her arguments. A high level of excitement can block thought as well as memory.

Remembering Songs and Poems

Songs and poems can be enjoyed in a number of different personal ways. Two of the more obvious ways are memorizing and concentrating on meaning, which, together with feeling and appreciation, can enhance your enjoyment.

Earlier in the book we mentioned the phenomenon of the serial position effect. This means that memory seems to function best at the beginning and the end, and tends to function less well in the middle. You will have more "beginnings" and "endings" if you memorize one section or stanza at a time. There are exceptions to this, of course, as you will discover for yourself. On the whole though, it is an excellent way to commit a poem or song to memory. Sometimes a narrative doesn't lend itself to memorization stanza by stanza. In that case you will memorize in a way that suits you best.

The following poem is by Walter Malone. It consists of four stanzas and is rather difficult. Here are some suggestions to help you memorize it. First, read it a few times in a relaxed state of mind. Fully absorb and appreciate and share the emotion the poet wants to arouse in you. Get a feeling for the rhythm, which will automatically remind you of the words and their meaning. Now you are ready to associate the lines together. A verbal association, using the rhyming words, would be helpful. Or you could chain the leading words together, such as, *laugh — like judgments seal — but never bind.* ... Or you can use the rhymes as natural associations, such as, weep/deep; I can/ man. If you have said the poem aloud a few times, these key words will be of great help in remembering. Do as much reciting aloud as possible; look at the poem if your memory fails — do it until it is no longer necessary.

OPPORTUNITY

They do me wrong who say I come no more,
When once I knock and fail to find you in;
For every day I stand outside your door
And bid you wake, and rise to fight and win.

Wail not for precious chances passed away;
Weep not for golden ages on the wane;
Each night I burn the records of the day;
At sunrise every soul is born again.

Laugh like a boy at splendors that have sped;
To vanished joys be blind and deaf and dumb;
My judgments seal the dead past with its dead,
But never bind a moment yet to come.

Though deep in mire, wring not your hands and weep;
I lend my arm to all who say, "I can";
No shamefaced outcast ever sank so deep,
But yet might rise and be again a man!

Try to answer these questions without referring to the poem:

1. To what or whom does "I" refer in the first line of the poem?
2. According to the writer, how often does opportunity come to you?
3. What takes place every night and every morning at sunrise, as indicated in the poem?
4. To whom does opportunity give aid?
5. Underline the word below that best indicates the feeling aroused by the poem.

surprise sorrow shame courage uncertainty

Remembering Theatrical Lines

Usually the director of a play schedules an adequate number of rehearsals to insure that all members of the cast have memorized their lines well. The only problem, insofar as memory is concerned, is if nervousness or stage fright should set in, causing temporary mental blanks.

Mental blanks on stage often occur just before the performer must speak, during a lengthy soliloquy.

Memorizing simple visual associations, pairing the performer's *first line* with the immediately preceding line — i.e. the last line of the preceeding speaker — can rectify this situation. Just a key word from each of the two sentences may be used as the cues.

Remembering in Athletics

Perhaps the most spectacular demonstration of communication, cooperation, control, and coordination is achieved when literally thousands of nerves, muscles, and chemicals join forces in the successful execution of a golf swing or a dance step. It would take a book to describe in detail how each component part performs its function in perfectly timed sequence.

The brain is responsible for coordinating and controlling all of these nerves, chemicals, and muscles. The execution of skilled movements is a mental as well as a physical activity. A skilled movement, properly executed, is knowledge. It requires learning. When the person is called upon to perform, successful recall is necessary. To enhance both learning and memory of any movement, the person engages in repetition or practice.

We can see then that skilled movements in athletics or related areas are partly a function of memory, and subject to the principles of forgetting discussed in Chapter 2.

Consider the memory problems of this young woman. She is learning to play tennis and is preparing to hit a basic forehand shot right after receiving instruction. She may have learned well enough how to swing correctly during practice, that is, without the ball being sent to her. But now comes "the moment of truth." The ball is about to be hit to her. Lacking confidence, she frantically tries to tell herself what to do by reviewing the instructor's words. She tells herself to keep her arm extended, to transfer the weight from her right to her left foot, to meet the ball slightly in front of her and so on. Then the ball is hit, rather easily and in perfect position, but what transpires looks more like a karate chop than a forehand. We can assume that she simply forgot the proper form when the ball was hit to her.

Problems of recall in relation to body movements confront a great many athletes when they are under pressure or in competitive situations. Basketball players, from school yard to professionals, shoot less accurately on foul shots in games than they do in practice. They score lower percentages because in actual games their bodily recall is subject to interference, which is caused by distraction and tension.

We can therefore regard comparatively poor performance of complex body movements under certain conditions as a memory problem and deal with it according to two principles discussed in Chapter 2: visualization and ego involvement.

Let's construct a situation that would use these two principles. You as a golfer approach the tee and prepare to recall. You do this by visualizing the correct procedure and not by repeating any instruction to yourself. You visualize the correct swing in its entirety, from the backswing to the follow-through. You are sure of your recall because if any part of the proper motion is left out, your visualization will not look right.

Now comes the principle of ego involvement. We remember things that happen to us very clearly. Thus as a golfer, you visualize yourself taking the correct swing. You do so from two points of view. First, you visualize yourself as a spectator, and then you visualize how you will look when you swing. You even try to remember what it feels like to swing correctly and by this means activate the kinesthetic aspect.

And being human, you are apt to remember your successes rather than your·failures and are likely to include a ball in your visualization. You see yourself swing perfectly, make perfect contact with the ball, and then see the ball take off for a beautiful shot. Basically, the same principles apply to any act of skill, especially one which does not require a partner or an opponent to exercise it.

Remembering Numbers

Associating events, people, or objects with numbers in an effort to remember quantities, dates, or places is probably the most difficult of the memory tasks. The problem is compounded by the fact that numbers are abstract. Can you picture "two"? You would have to ask, "two what?" If the answer is two apples, a picture is possible, but if the number is 200 apples, the thought is abstract again.

Obviously, if we are to remember numbers for whatever reason, we should not try to remember them in their present form. We must convert the number to something that is familiar and concrete, something that can easily be visualized and associated.

As a warm-up exercise, try to memorize the ten words below in order. Do not try to remember by repeating the sequence to yourself. Instead, form a chain of associations. Visualize each word and associate it a visual chain that makes a story. Your story may be as wild and ridiculous as your mind can create. Also, put yourself in the story. You start off by seeing yourself riding on a mare. The mare steps on a mat. You take it from there. After you have completed your story, test yourself.

mare, mat, suit, gun, light, rag, dear, sail, case, bear

If you concentrated and chained all ten words together, you probably remembered all of them. If so, congratulations! You just memorized a twenty-digit number. The number is 37,345,462,147,692,510,587. You were able to succeed because each of the words is a representation of a two-digit number. We now arrive at the system which provides for the conversion of numbers into familiar and easily visualized words.

First let us have each number transformed into a letter for the following reasons:

0 = k   *O* and *k* are often associated, such as in "okay" and "K.O."

1 = l   The small letter *l* and *1* look alike.

2 = n   Turn the *2* sideways and it looks something like *n*.

3 = m   These are also alike for the same reason.

4 = t   The small *t* would look like a *4* but for one missing line.

5 = s   They are almost alike.

6 = g   These also look quite similar. A soft *g* or *j* sound can also be used.

7 = r   If the small *r* were turned around and straightened out just a bit.

8 = b or p   A *p* on top of a *b* would make an *8*. (Well, sort of.)

9 = d   A *9* turned upside down becomes a *d*.

From here the procedure is simple. By merely combining two of these letters and inserting a vowel sound between them you can formulate words designating any number from O to 99.

Suppose you wish to make the number 85. You would have a *b*, the letter conversion for 8 on the left-hand side of the number, and hence, on the left-hand side of the word. The letter for 5, an *s*, would be on the right. Now put a vowel sound in the middle. What word can you make? If you try the *a* sound first, you will come up with the word *base*. What word would you make for 62? *Gun* would be a good one, though *jean* and *gin* could also be used. *Gone* would have fit, but that would be somewhat of an abstract word. It is hard to visualize *gone*. Now suppose you are recalling a vision, and in this vision you see *rain*. What number are you recalling? The answer is 72. What number is a *bomb?* The answer is 83. Only the sounds count. Thus the silent *b* has no numerical value. The same is true of the *c* in *talk* which makes 40.

Vowels should be chosen by thinking of the order: *a, e, i, o, u*. You would normally choose the first concrete word that can be formed with *a*, then try *e*, and so on. *Rake* would be used for 70 rather than *rock*.

On page 95 is a chart of the word conversions from 1 through 99. Notice that the numbers 1 through 9 are treated if they had a zero in front of them.

TABLE OF CONVERSIONS

0		10		20		30		40	
0	CAKE	10	LAKE	20	NECK	30	MIKE	40	TACK
1	COAL	11	LILY	21	NAIL	31	MAIL	41	TAIL
2	CANE	12	LANE	22	NUM	32	MINE	42	TIN
3	COMB	13	LAMB	23	NUMB	33	MAMA	43	TOMB
4	CAT	14	LIGHT	24	GNAT	34	MAT	44	TOT
5	CASE	15	LACE	25	NEICE	35	MICE	45	TOES
6	KEG	16	LEG	26	NAG	36	MIG	46	TAG
7	CAR	17	LAIR	27	NERO	37	MARE	47	TEAR
8	CAP	18	LAB	28	KNOB	38	MOB	48	TUB
9	COD	19	LAD	29	NOD	39	MAID	49	TIDE

50		60		70		80		90	
50	SACK	60	JACK	70	RAKE	80	BEAK	90	DIKE
51	SAIL	61	GOAL	71	RAIL	81	BULL	91	DIAL
52	SUN	62	GUN	72	RAIN	82	BEAN	92	DEAN
53	PSALM	63	GUM	73	RAM	83	BOMB	93	DAME
54	SUIT	64	GATE	74	RAT	84	BAT	94	DATE
55	SISSY	65	GOOSE	75	ROSE	85	BASE	95	DICE
56	SAGE	66	GAG	76	RAG	86	BAG	96	DOG
57	SORE	67	GEAR	77	REAR	87	BEAR	97	DEER
58	SOAP	68	JEEP	78	RIB	88	BABY	98	DOPE
59	SEED	69	GIDDY	79	REED	89	BEAD	99	DEED

Below is a list of ten tasks. Use the conversions from 1 through 10 and you will see how easy it is to remember them in the proper sequence.

1. Clean the floor.
2. Write a letter.
3. Go to the doctor.
4. Buy theater tickets.
5. Do the laundry.
6. Mail a birthday card.
7. Wash the car.
8. Return a library book.
9. Cook dinner.
10. Water the flowers.

To remember each task in sequence, associate the task with the converted word. For number 1, associate *floor* with the word *coal* (01). Forming a good picture of coal on a floor will suffice. For number 2, picture a letter being written with a cane. For number 3, you see your doctor combing his hair. Now memorize the rest on your own and test yourself.

Throughout the list you can see that certain key words can be used as cues. "Theater tickets" or simply "tickets" for number 4 would be sufficient to enable you to recall the entire task. If, in actual practice, you remember a birthday card but still cannot remember what to do with the birthday card, you surely have quite a problem! Ninety-nine percent of the time that you forget a task, you will notice that it is the type that *"completely* slips your mind." A partial slip is very rare indeed. Therefore, one word in each phrase suffices to recall all that you wish. This principle is important for remembering facts. So much of memory is just finding that starting point.

The conversion system has countless uses in practical life. Remembering things to do, shopping lists, dates, phone numbers, and catalog prices can be facilitated by the system. The phone number 724-2851 can be remembered by associating the converted words *car, gnat, mob,* and *sail* in a visual chain. The invention of the steamboat associates the streamboat with a car (07). (Notice that when remembering dates, in most instances, you will normally have enough knowledge at your disposal to be able to drop the first two digits.)

Academically, you will find the system useful anytime a number must be remembered, such as formulas and historic dates. Let's take just four examples here. Most people start having trouble remembering presidents when they reach Andrew Jackson, the seventh president. We shall start with the eighth, then, Martin Van Buren. First, picture a van with a bureau in it. This is your cue. Then associate with *cab*. Perhaps you see a cab pulling the van. The ninth president was William Henry Harrison. There are several movie stars by that name. You may use one such visual image as the cue, or perhaps you know someone personally by that name. In either case, you visualize that person holding a codfish (09). The tenth is John Tyler. Imagine a tire floating in a lake (10). James K. Polk? How is *pole* for a cue? If that is okay, then imagine a lily growing out of a pole. Now if you are asked the eighth president of the United States, you first turn to your picture of a cab. You will then see not only the cab, but a van with a bureau in it as well. The data must still be processed just as a computer must process its retrieved information to arrive at a solution to a problem. You must then ask yourself what the retrieved data, van and bureau, and mean. Only a complete lack of knowledge of the subject would cause you to give *van bureau* as your answer.

If you later wish to use the word conversions for something else, the old associations can be erased by the new ones almost as easily as is done on a tape recorder. The system can be quite flexible.

At this point you can use your knowledge of fact association and numerical conversion to try this exercise. Your objective is to be able to remember the facts concerning the reproductions of famous works of art on pages 98–101.

In each case you are to remember the title of the painting, the artist's name, and the artist's dates or the year in which the work was executed.

Start by picking out some object in a painting, for example — any special or unique feature it possesses. Visualize that feature in isolation and connect cues for the names of the paintings and the artists. Now add your conversion to the chain. Whether or not art is your interest, this will be a good mental exercise.

The Conversion System in Business

The conversion system has endless possibilities in business life. It could be applied to this situation in which a real estate saleswoman ruefully explained her predicament with the following illustrations. Mr. and Mrs. Customer walk through the door explaining they need a four-bedroom house in the $40,000 range. Although the sales-

Walt Whitman, by John White Alexander (1856–1915)

Gas, by Edward Hopper (1882–1967)

Still Life with Apples, by Paul Cezanne (1839–1906)

At the Milliner's, by Edgar Degas (1834–1917)

Pepito Costa y Bonells, by Francesco de Goya (1746-1828)

Stag with Blue Palms,
(1967)
by Jesse Allen

Ancestral Moon Dance,
(1974)
by Michael Bower

woman has seen countless houses, she cannot recall and describe a house that would be suitable for this couple. She therefore goes through the usual procedure — she checks the files. Eventually, she finds a house that fits her client's description.

They drive off, perhaps traveling several miles to see the house. If the customers are not satisfied, they must return to the office to check the files once more. Needless to say, there must be a more efficient way to conduct a sale.

Much of this inefficiency could be avoided by making a list of houses to look at. From the standpoint of sales psychology, this would be inadvisable. A customer would surely want to see *all* the houses on the list, and after spending an entire afternoon might very well be too confused to make a decision that day. And getting a customer to come back another day might result in losing the sale.

A more favorable atmosphere would be one in which the saleswoman could almost immediately say, "Oh yes, I have the house for you," and then give a brief description. Later, if the customers are not satisfied with the first house, the saleswoman might say, "Okay, I have another house, also with four bedrooms, in the same price range. It has ..." Talking about the house from memory carries a personal touch, which is much better than reading from a file card. The saleswoman must have a system that will enable her to reach into her mental storage area and re-trive information about the most suitable house for any customer.

Before we describe the procedure that the saleswoman now uses, let's start with one basic premise — any sequence of ideas, or experiences, or faces, can in large part be recalled if you can first remember what is most important, what is unique. The key idea that the saleswoman selects for association would be the best physical feature of a house — the main selling point. If she can recall this physical feature, other recollections will soon follow.

The next step is to associate that key feature with a number. She reserves numbers 1 to 10 for one-bedroom houses, with the cheapest price tag, $14,000, being accorded number 1, and so on to the most expensive, say $50,000, which she accords number 10. She does the same for two-bedroom houses, using numbers 11 to 30; three-bedroom houses get 31 to 50; four-bedroom get 51 to 70, five get 71 to 85, and six and above are reserved for the remaining word conversions.

Now the saleswoman is showing a house which has just been listed for sale by her office. It is a four-bedroom house and costs $40,000. She associated the word conversion for 60 (Jack) to the key feature, which is a very large enclosed front porch (Jack on the porch).

Why does she use the number 60? Well, any four-bedroom house will have a number between 51 and 70, with the highest price in that category being associated with 70, and the lowest getting 51. Since she decides that $40,000 is about the median price for four-bedroom homes, it would fall midway between 51 and 70. (Remember that we are talking about relative price, not actual price). Next, using number conversions and cues, the saleswoman chains the address of the house to the association of Jack and the porch.

Now, when Mr. and Mrs. Customer describe what they are looking for, the saleswoman can immediately refer to her word conversions. If the customer needs a four-bedroom house in the $40,000 range, she scans the numbers from 59 through 61. These word conversions will connect to key features of four-bedroom houses in the clients' price range. Each in turn is isolated mentally.

When the saleswoman gets to "Jack" she will see a large, lovely porch, and an association for the address. Once the porch is pictured, other things will be recalled about the house. She then says, "I have just the house for you. Come, I'll tell you about it on the way."

Notice one of the main techniques here — organization. The words were then connected according to that organization. Notice also that success in using the word conversion system lies mainly in knowing the words backwards, forwards, and inside out. It would be a travesty to make a large number of associations and then forget the words themselves at the time of recall.

Learning the Words

The words can be learned with amazingly little effort. Once you know the basic system behind the formation of the words, you can, and should, make up your own chart. You can compare yours with the words I have used and make adjustments if you wish. If you come up with words different from mine, it may be a good idea to use them as long as the basic system is followed, and that for a given number you consistently use the same word. The point is that if you construct the words yourself, you will remember your own construction better than if you tried remembering someone else's. After you have done this, recite the words to yourself a few times, or better still, use them at every opportunity. Go shopping, and remember 40 items by association each to the first 40 words.

Some Quick Ways of Remembering Numbers

There may be occasions when you do not have time to form associations, or you wish to retain the numbers only long enough to use them right away or write them down. The following suggestions will be helpful:

1. You may find organization or progression in numbers (see Chapter 2). Can you see the organization in the Social Security number: 059-32-5969? Almost any number can be more firmly committed to memory if you are aware of how the numbers relate to each other.

2. You can perform a mental operation (the thought principle) on the numbers by adding them up. Or you can use a combination of addition and organization. For example, take the telephone number 587-6419. You add the left and right sides up and get 20 for each. Later on you will remember your mental operation. You may not recall immediately where and what all the numbers were, but your memory for the totals might be just the starting point that you need. From there you may suddenly be reminded of the entire number (as often happens in the case where the number has been used several

times before, but for that moment is unavailable for recall). Or you may find yourself remembering that it started with a 5 and ended with a 9. Then if you remind yourself of the totals, and mentally toss some figures around in your head, it is possible that the others will fall into place.

3. Visualize the numbers in three dimensions and vivid color.

4. Divide numbers into dollars and cents. The zip code 15227 can be more easily remembered as $152.27.

5. Some numbers can be thought of as a date, e.g., 1957, 1546.

6. You can use a variation of the conversion system by changing each number to a letter and making a word. The phone number 329-5073 can be committd to memory as M I N D S C R A M, or 3908 and Many Damn Cars Go Backward, or 877-8155 as Barry Blass. This methods is tremendously effective. Try it!

Remembering Names and Faces

We shall deal with what is probably the most common cause of complaints about memory — names and faces. People in business and industry, from secretaries to top executives, will be the first to agree that the ability to remember names can be of tremendous benefit.

You must be convinced that it is as important to remember a person's name as it is to be introduced to him. You must also be willing to give the introduction your complete attention. Unfortunately, many people are often too busy thinking of a conversational item when they should be listening to the introduction. So be sure to give your full attention to an introduction.

In giving your full attention, don't be afraid to show that the person's name is important to you. If the person is introducing himself (or herself), get a clear picture of his face and the way his lips move. Later, if you are not sure of remembering the face, you will very likely forget the name that goes with it. However, a visual picture of the moment of the introduction will give you an extra path to recall. A visual picture would include the person's expression, his posture, what he was wearing, and any other aspect of his personality.

The mind does most of its forgetting shortly after learning. Interference is most potent right after we hear a person's name for the first time. It's too bad that those moments immediately following an introduction are usually taken up with speaking as well as listening.

The implication here is obvious. You must review a name shortly after you first hear it and be alert for an opportunity to use the name in the ensuing conversation. By acquiring the habit of saying, "How do you do, Mr. _____ (or Mrs. _____ or Miss _____)," you will substantially increase your ability to remember.

You will also need to use the principle of discrimination. One of New York's foremost artists once told me of her difficulty in remembering faces, especially when she would briefly encounter someone at an art gallery or at a meeting.

My friend was not so much concerned with remembering a name as she was with simply being able to recognize people and not offend by failing to say hello. I suggested that when she meets someone whom she fails to recognize, she might make believe that she is drawing a caricature of him. As we know, in a caricature the artist selects and exaggerates a characteristic feature of a person. To do so entails a process of discrimination. This procedure worked for the artist and it will help you too.

During an introduction, we are generally given both the first and last names. Because of the unrelated nature of the information, the mind unconsciously senses difficulty and even tends to reject it. Rarely, if ever, would we need to remember both names right away. Depending upon the social situation, we might remember either the first or last name, but just the act of selecting one of the two names for special mental attention enhances retention.

However, our objective is to consider methods that will make us experts in remembering names. We would like you to develop the skill that will enable you to meet ten or more people during an evening and remember all then names. Let's begin.

The Basic Method: Make the Person Fit the Name

If people were named Tall, Fatty, and Ugly, we would have no difficulty remembering their names because their physical appearance would remind us of them. Similarly, if people were named Engineer, Smart Aleck, or Cheapskate, we would also perceive relationships, especially if we knew something about them.

Such convenient relationships are rarely encountered in everyday life, but if we are alert, we can find some. We might meet a man named Short who is a little over five feet tall, or a man who loves to fish named Fischer, or a woman with an extremely red face named Burns. Once we see the relationship, the technique is easy. We simply verbalize the relationship to ourselves by saying, Mrs. Burns is so named because she has such a red face. Later, her red face will remind you of her name.

As we said, these relationships exist only rarely. A person named Burns will usually have a normal complexion. Mr. Taylor may not be a tailor, and Mr. Blue will certainly not look blue. In the more common situations, where no relationship exists, why not create a relationship? Unleash your imagination. If Mr. Blue is not colored blue, you may solve the problem by looking at him and making him blue. As he is introduced, you perform the mental operation of coloring him blue. Get a very clear picture in your mind of the man and imagine him with a deep blue face. Later, in recall, on seeing his face, you will be reminded of the word *blue* because his face and the color will become associated in your mind.

This is easier said than done. It takes a lot of practice, and when you practice, you must make sure that you really concentrate on performing the mental operations. On page 108 are the pictures of four people. Focus your attention on number 1. His name is Mr. Green. Make him green in your mind's eye. Now focus on number 2. His name is Mr. Gunn. You can imagine him holding a gun.

1

2

3

4

Number 3 is Mrs. Grimsby. You can think of her as looking very grim. Number 4, Miss Stone — her face is so hard-looking that it is easy for you to imagine a stone.

Now test your recall and look at the same faces in scrambled order on page 110. Focus your attention on each one. Relax, and perhaps the associations will come back to you. If they do not, don't be discouraged. It takes confidence and practice to do this.

You may feel that this technique works fine for names like Lyons, Kapp, Cohen, Burger, Rose, Sugar, Brown, Fischer, Carpenter, Coates, Fox, and Wolfe. But what about names that aren't similar to a concrete word that you can visualize? For these, select cues. A cue is easily associated and remembered, and when it is recalled, it will serve to remind you of the complete name. Let the word *green* be a cue for the name Greenfield. If you can look at the person and be reminded of the word *green*, this will in turn remind you of the name Greenfield. If recall does not occur instantly, you can mentally transport yourself back to the moment when you were introduced. You picture yourself saying, "How do you do, Mr. Green . . . Green . . . Green . . . ?" and then the name Greenfield is retrieved.

Let's consider associations as cues. *Gun* is a cue for the name Gunther. You may be worried about the possibility of meeting this man later and saying, "Hello, Mr. Gun." This won't happen if you complete the connection by saying, "How do you do, Mr. Gunther?" Using your other associations now, you can easily see that *grim* could be a cue for the name Grimsby. If you have to recall the name Bellson, for example, a picture in your mind of a man ringing a bell will usually remind you of the full name.

The Pitfall — Mental Inhibitions

As you may well imagine, not all of your associations will be flattering to the person whose name you wish to remember. In fact, most associations may very well be downright insulting. You must not let this interfere with

your mental construction and creativity. No one has to know what is in your mind. I recall a Mrs. Schwartz who was both amazed and flattered that I had remembered her name after a two-year interval. She had no way of knowing that I was aided greatly by my mental picture of a gigantic wart in the middle of her chin.

A suggestion: Make the association with the first thing that comes to your mind. This is a book on memory, not on how to make friends.

An Alternate Method

In some instances the following method for remembering names will be superior to the one previously discussed because associations can be drawn more quickly and because the associations are strictly internal. This method will work very well when you meet a large number of people at the same time — at a party, a new job, a business meeting.

This is essentially a matter of discrimination. Pick something that stands out or is unique about the person. Preferably, select a physical feature, such as a large mop of hair, or big blue eyes. However, if you cannot think of something outstanding, an article of clothing will do. Then connect your selection to the name and isolate the association. A few examples will illustrate the technique. You are introduced to a person who has very big blue eyes. The name is Blankenship. You isolate the blue eyes and place them on a ship. (Notice that the face is not included in your association). You see another wearing a bright green tie. The name is Carney. So, you picture a tie on a car. A person has big ears and the name is Gibson. Visualize big ears on someone you know, or on a famous person named Gibson. You can see that this method will work well for common names that are difficult to associate.

Later on, when you see the person again and wish to recall his name, ask yourself what object or feature you selected. Your selection will be retrieved with remarkable ease. You visualize just the blue eyes and notice that they are on a ship. If you repeat the name shortly after the introduction, a ship will recall the image of the man Blankenship. Visualizing the green tie and big ears will produce the names Carney and Gibson respectively.

No method is completely foolproof, and this method has some drawbacks. If you use as your selection an article of clothing, recall will be difficult after a period of time because the person will most likely be wearing different clothes. But perhaps you can still remember by evoking a mental picture of the original introduction. If you can remember what the person was wearing then, you can remember your selection and recall the association of that selection. If you use a more permanent feature, such as a big nose or bushy eyebrows, interference may result, since many people have such features, and the same selections could be used over and over again. On the other hand, this method is usually faster, since you normally have time to select a feature before the introduction, and thus have half the connection ready.

Perhaps the best way to use this method is to make a drawing of these quick associations and then pick a time to review them. Reviewing can be accomplished by looking at each drawing and testing yourself to see if you can recall the selection you made, the association, and then the name. If the procedures were properly performed, you could review ten or fifteen names in a minute or two. Try to review without resorting to the associations, or better still, try to use the name in conversation. With usage, you can retain the name.

Comparing the Methods

In order to resolve any confusion about Method One and Method Two, let's illustrate their difference by using the name Geiger. With Method One, you try to associate the person with the name Geiger. Perhaps you picture him with a Geiger counter. With Method Two, you pick out some concrete feature of the person and associate only that feature with a Geiger counter. If the man has red hair, you would picture a Geiger counter with red hair. Although Method Two is useful for meeting a large number of people in a short time, and Method One is useful for a more ordinary situation with fewer people, you can use either method, depending on your personal preference.

Combining the Methods

Very often you can modify your method by treating your selection as part of a descriptive process. In that case, you would really be combining both methods. Let's take an easy example. Suppose you select freckles as a man's outstanding feature and you are told his name is Pat. You would picture yourself (note the principle of ego involvement) patting the freckles. If the man's name were Gunther, you would picture yourself shooting him in the feature you selected. In other words, you can picture anything the name describes as happening to the outstanding feature.

Remembering First Names

First names can be remembered by using either Method One or Method Two. Because we generally use first names more often, you can apply still another method to connect a name and a face.

On hearing someone introduced as Jim, you can immediately think of the first "Jim" that comes to your mind. Then notice just how much of the "new Jim" resembles the "other Jim." Here you can again use your imagination — you can always find some feature that is common to both Jims. Just the act of searching the face and selecting that feature will help memory. If there's not an ounce of resemblance, you can verbalize this to yourself — an opposite association can be quite effective. Later on, in recall, you look at the man and you will notice just how much he resembles (or does not resemble) the man you know named Jim. That will be your trigger for recall.

Remembering a Long Sequence of Names

The technique of recognizing and forming associations works well, but you may ask, "What happens when you are introduced to a large number of people in rapid succession?"

Picture a meeting at which the chairman introduces eight people. He says, "This is Mr. Hilary," and with barely a second's pause between each introduction, "This is Mr. Gardner, Mr. Franklin, Mrs. Ackerman, Mr. Kirkland, Mr. Metzer, Mrs. Alexander, and Mr. Salvadore." You hardly have time to extend a hand and certainly little or no chance to form associations. Actually, you can find relationships with surprising quickness, as long as you have creativity, self-confidence, and most of all, have acquired practice. Yet it must be admitted that for the average beginner, this way of introducing people can adversely affect all attempts at associating.

Bear in mind that your primary objective in learning how to remember names is to be able to first remember a single name on introduction. If you can reach a level of proficiency where you can remember one or two names every five minutes or so, while you are functioning normally during the intervals, your study and practice will have been well rewarded. Remembering a long sequence of names is easy if you have taken note of the particular circumstances, such as a gathering at dinner, or the physical surroundings. It may not be necessary for you to associate a name with a face, but rather with the particular place or circumstance. Suppose the eight people mentioned above are seated around a table and the chairman, starting from left to right, introduces Mr. Hilary first. Immediately, you envision *yourself* on a hill. Mr. Gardner is next, and you see a garden on top of the hill. When Mr. Franklin is introduced, you may imagine Benjamin Franklin flying his kite in that garden, and so on, for the remaining five people.

Now you have all the material you need to recall the names of the individuals around the table. To recall the third person, you go through the chain and stop at the third association. Of course, this method is really a trick. If you met the person the next day, or in fact anywhere other than in his original position, you would be in trouble. Consequently, you must build upon the original association as soon as you have the chance.

After you have gathered your story chain together, review it, focusing your mind on each person as you reach that person's association. Perhaps at this point you could use the time to find better associations, connecting the person, or the particulars of that person, to the name. The original story chain should not be completely forgotten, however. It may come in handy even when you are trying to recall in some entirely different situation. In your attempt to focus on each person while reviewing the story chain, you will be able to remember just where everyone stood or sat, and then recall the association for that particular situation.

Remembering a Short Sequence of Names

We are not often required to remember a sequence of six or more names, remembering even three or four can be a problem. A letter chain will usually work wonders. Seated around a table are Carl, Alice, Laura, and Tom. Quickly you would think of CALT and silently make the sound. When you have a free moment, review the group. In such a situation, your associations can be familiar initials of organizations or meaningless words. This method is effective for small groups.

Remembering Those Little Things to Do

We have all had the experience of forgetting to bring some item, or to relay a message, or to turn off at a particular exit. This is what we mean by "forgetting the little things."

Perhaps these "little things" do not really constitute forgetting. Forgetting occurs when we consciously make an effort to remember and we fail. Here the problem may be one of timing. We were busy thinking of something else. Perhaps we were talking while passing the exit at which we should have turned. Let's consider the high school student who is about to play in his first varsity basketball game and who upon getting dressed realizes that he has "forgotten" to bring his sneakers. Surely the young fellow knew that he needed sneakers for basketball. It simply did not occur to him, and he did not think of the sneakers at the proper time. His forgetting really represents a problem in what might be called "personal organization."

Because we are accustomed to associating these errors in timing with memory, and because forgetting "little things" plagues all of us, the principles already touched on can help us to alleviate them.

Memory and Personal Organization

We have seen how principle and organization are important in remembering what we read and what we hear. Organization is related to all aspects of successful mental functioning. It is no coincidence that people who describe themselves as disorganized also say that they are forgetful.

It's easy to understand why the organized person is less likely to forget things. He has unwittingly acquired the habit of applying principles of memory. For example, the organized person makes a list of things that must be done by a given day or week. The list will often start with the most important chore and gradually work down to the least important. The mere act of mental discrimination, which decides the relative importance of each chore, aids memory. Furthermore, writing utilizes the kinesthetic faculty and provides an extra avenue for recall. After these mental and physical operations, a person may not even meed the list anymore.

Remembering by Categorizing

We now understand that personal organization affects memory. The individual whose daily life is well organized is less likely to forget than the one who lacks organization.

Personal organization varies among individuals. The differences are a matter of degree. Even the most disorganized person possesses *some* sense of organization.

How often do we have the feeling that we have forgotten a task, and yet no matter how hard we try we just cannot remember it. We might ask ourselves, "Could our forgetting have anything to do with our job? If thinking about our job does not stir our memory, we may then ask ourselves if our forgetting has something to do with our family, or our social life, or our material possessions.

These categories can be mentally subdivided into further components. After deciding to search the "family" component, we can ask ourselves if the forgotten task has anything to do with our spouse, our children, or our parents. The components of the "material possessions" category would include our car, the house, and clothes, for example. When each category is isolated in our mind for a few brief but powerful seconds, correct recall will almost always occur.

How and When to Categorize Your Thoughts

Suppose Mr. Businessman is about to leave his office. As his hand touches the door knob, something reminds him that he must make an important telephone call. He makes the call and is thankful that he "remembered." Now suppose this man is in the comfort of his home. It is after business hours — too late to make a business call. Suddenly, the recollection of a phone call comes to him. What does he say to himself? You guessed it — "I forgot!" This despite the fact that the earlier and the later recollections were the same, the only difference being that of *time* and *place*. Whether or not we forget to do something often depends on when and where we "remember." Sometimes when we remember things too late we call it "forgetting," when actually we failed to organize our thoughts properly.

From the standpoint of memory, some moments are more important than others, and we must be sure to remember during those moments. For many people those important moments are just before leaving home in the morning or just before going home in the evening. If we remember at those moments, we'll do whatever we have to do; otherwise, we'll forget. It is precisely during these moments that we should acquire the habit of organizing our thoughts to make sure that we have not forgotten anything. The fifteen seconds or so that it may take to do this will be well worth the effort.

Remembering for the Future

A large part of our remembering relates to the future. We need to turn off the parkway at a certain exit as we begin our trip. We want to make sure that we will give our co-worker an important report before, and not after he (or she) leaves for the day. We say things like, "Sure, I'll call you tomorrow night" — and we don't. We'll discuss how you can follow through with your intentions.

Memories come back to us through mental associations. An object we are looking at now, or an event that is taking place now, can remind us of something that took place in the past and triggers a stream of memories. Or we are reminded of something we failed to do in the past by something we are doing now. This doesn't *always* happen, but it is helpful when it does.

Suppose we continue to regard the forgetting of little things to do as errors of timing. Forgetting to turn off at the desired exit on the parkway occurs simply because you were not thinking of it at the right time. What is needed is some object that will appear before the exit you want and jog your memory.

Imagine yourself driving along the parkway and running into a very heavy traffic jam caused by a serious accident. Because of the jam you must turn off the highway at a certain exit. Do you think you will be reminded of all that happened the next time you approach the same place? Most likely you will, and you will turn off the parkway at the same exit.

And yet you need not experience a real traffic jam to make sure that you turn off at a particular exit. You can create the experience yourself, by visualizing it, using vivid color, exaggeration, and all your imagination. If you are at all familiar with the road, you can imagine the accident occurring at a specific point. A bridge, a tunnel, a park, appearing just before the exit will serve as a reminder. Well in advance of your approach to the exit, and just as you come to the landmark, you will be reminded of the accident, and you will make the correct turn.

You can create an experience to remember anything as long as you know in advance what you want to remember. Suppose you want to make sure you give a co-worker some written information. You create an incident, the more exaggerated and improbable the better. You can picture your co-worker receiving the written information, getting red in the face, pounding the desk, and saying out loud, "My God, how I needed this! Do you know what might have happened if I didn't get it?" You then picture your co-worker fainting, and you calling a doctor. Later, the moment you see the person, you will be reminded of the incident as you pictured it in your mind, and you will remember to give him the paper.

To summarize the procedure: First, decide what it is you want to remember. Then pick out some object, or place, or person closely associated in time and place. Finally, create some unlikely incident in which that object, place, or person is a central element. To make the technique slightly more effective, you might relate these steps to an actual desired task, although this is not really necessary.

Remembering a Large Number of Tasks

Whether in a business or social situation, some of us need to recall a large number of tasks — say four or five — each day. In these circumstances, it may be time-consuming and mentally frustrating to create memories for every little task, but you can still utilize the technique of creating incidents that serve to snap your mind back to the desired task at the right time. Simply imagine yourself performing each task in the exact environment at precisely the same moment that you expect to perform the task — but omit the "extras." In other words, if you want to give a co-worker a report, simply imagine yourself giving it. Imagine all the circumstances as you expect them to be. You will surely remember later, even if the circumstances are slightly different.

Discriminating When and Where to Remember

Which statement do you think will be easier to remember: (a) Take this pill once every day, or (b) Take this pill after every meal. The correct answer is *b* because the meal will be a reminder. Not having a definite time and place can cause you to forget. But if you know exactly when and where you are to perform a task, the factors of time and place will of themselves help you to remember. Clearly, if the task does not specify a definite time and place, we must. We must state *exactly when* and *exactly where* we will make the phone call, or mail the letter. The mere act of discriminating will sharply reduce your chances of forgetting.

Remembering Where You Put Things

Talking to yourself as you are putting an object in place can be helpful. It is also helpful to have a reason for putting an object in a particular place and verbalizing the fact. But even if you don't have a special reason, it will help to make one up. For example, say out loud, "I am placing the baby pictures on the dresser because it is near the crib."

Your own body motions will also help you to remember. When you put something in a particular place, make an extra motion, or give the object an extra flip. If you put something in a lower drawer, give it a little kick to close. If you are alone, you have nothing to worry about. If on the other hand there is someone with you, you can close the drawer with the back of your hand, or you can place a letter on the table with a gentle pat instead of a big slap. Later, while visualizing an object you put somewhere, you will also be able to recall the place.

Remembering the Cards While Playing

Under normal circumstances, remembering the cards that have been played is not as difficult as it seems. It is largely a matter of concentration. It is impossible to close your eyes and think of absolutely nothing. With your eyes open, however, if you have nothing special or particular to look at, your mind can go blank. You would remember much more if you kept your mind active and related it to specific objects — such as the cards while playing. Sometimes it may not be easy to maintain full concentration on the cards. In poker, for instance, it is easy to be distracted by thoughts of money. Then consider the bridge player who has a queer feeling that she is botching her play of the hand, while she worries that the kibitzer looking over her shoulder *knows* she is botching it. And she worries about what she'll say to her partner when the game is over. Well, recognize these side thoughts while playing, and get the habit of bringing your mind back to the game and the cards.

Remembering Friends and Relationships

It is a truism that to have a friend, you must be a friend. Similarly, if you want to get ideas across and influence people, you must be able to understand people.

Here is a typical situation: You are speaking to someone, a friend. Your friend becomes animated and enthusiastic while speaking to you. Suddenly, you become aware that you have not been listening. Your mind has been wandering — and your friend is aware of it and looks offended. As you part, you may say to yourself, "Okay, the next time we meet I will definitely show interest in what he is saying." You do show interest the next time. In fact, you show enthusiasm as you look directly at your friend's face and continue the conversation without blinking an eye. You haven't fooled him, however. Somehow he knows that when you say, "I see," you haven't really seen. And when you say, "Very interesting," you haven't found it at all interesting. Needless to say, you have not strengthened your relationship with your friend.

Lapses of attention are very common in ordinary conversation. Sometimes I think that the basis of most friendships is the tolerance people develop toward each other's wanderings. Most real friendships, however, are sustained when each concentrates on what the other is saying. It's not easy to do this without some effort. We will discuss concentration in the next chapter.

Memory is a necessary ingredient for sustaining friendships. When you say to a friend, "How is your son doing in medical school?" you are showing interest. It is therefore very helpful to remember personal facts about your friends and to use them in your relationships.

Summary

In this chapter we continued to explain and extend the use of the principles and techniques for developing your memory that were discussed earlier in the book.

There are an infinite number of problems and situations to which you can apply these principles and techniques. Since every situation in life is different, and every individual is different, you have endless opportunities to develop your memory, to improve your ability to concentrate, and in general to improve your mental capacity.

It is up to you to remain alert, to keep your mind active, and to draw on the creative reserves you possess.

Chapter Eight

CONCENTRATION — WHAT IT CAN DO FOR YOU

Are You Like This Man?

Let's take a look at Joe. He has a job but isn't doing very well at it. Somehow he's not alert or working at a pace that will earn him advancement. He wants to be more productive, but he can't because his mind wanders. Today, for example, a large part of his thoughts are centered around his eight-year-old boy who is having trouble in school. Later, at dinner, Joe engages in some aimless conversation, but his heart isn't in it.

After dinner, the boy asks Joe for help with his homework, and of course Joe says he will be glad to help. Within two minutes, however, something happens. The boy looks at his father and senses that his mind is elsewhere. Where? You guessed it. His mind is back on his problems with his job.

At this juncture, Joe's wife interrupts to suggest that they might go away for a weekend to relax. No chance! Joe wouldn't be able to relax. It may sound paradoxical, but a person who finds it hard to concentrate will also find it hard to relax and enjoy a rest.

You might say that Joe's plight is ridiculous. Doesn't he realize that with the same amount of mental effort he could be successful in his job, relate better to his son's problems, and enjoy a weekend with his family? That, in fact, he can be successful at whatever he undertakes? The only skill he needs is to stay mentally "with it" — to give complete attention to the right thing at the right time.

Who does Joe remind you of? Yourself, of course. Like Joe, we are all plagued, in varying degrees, with the problem of mind wandering. Let's learn why our minds wander and how we can remedy this.

What Is Concentration?

To concentrate means *"to focus, to fix one's attention,"* and *concentration* is "the act of focusing, of fixing one's attention." These definitions also apply in a nonpersonal sense. When a military commander masses all his forces and equipment opposite the enemy lines, we say that he has concentrated them for strong defense or attack.

It follows, then, that to concentrate effectively in our own minds, we must engage all our mental resources and faculties and focus them on a single chain of thought or piece of information.

Some people think that concentration implies a state of tension. No, it does not and it should not. In true concentration, the body is relaxed while the mind works and uses its resources to solve problems and deal with situations.

How Concentration Relates to Some of Our Problems

Let's consider the high school student who is taking an examination. He has prepared for the test, though perhaps not as thoroughly as he might. He should, nevertheless, be able to give a decent account of himself on the examination. When he looks at the test he sees a couple of tough questions, and suddenly he loses his ability to think clearly. At moments he even forgets the most elementary answers. In short, he has suffered what he thinks is "a mental blank" during the examination.

You know that the student hasn't suffered "a mental blank" at all. Perhaps "mental congestion" might be a better description. The student was probably thinking of what would happen if he failed, what his parents would say if he failed, what his friends would think if he failed — all sorts of thoughts that had nothing to do with the examination he was taking. He was not thinking of the right things at the right time.

Concentration and Making a Speech

Suppose you are standing on a platform, making a speech. Suddenly, you suffer "a mental blank" similar to that of the student taking the examination. You begin to worry about what will happen if you forget your speech and what the audience will do. This wouldn't happen if you didn't allow thoughts that had nothing to do with the subject of your speech to intrude.

The problem is one of self-consciousness, which in this case means that you are more conscious of your audience than of the subject matter of your speech, and you are worrying about what they think. Such thoughts will interfere with and inhibit your own spontaneous expression.

Concentration and Selling

Suppose you are a salesman or saleswoman. This is an occupation which, by its very nature, causes occasional lapses of memory or attention. Let's imagine you are talking to a customer and without being aware of it, you find yourself thinking, "I wonder if he is going to buy or not. If he buys a large quantity, it will mean X number of dollars in my pocket. ..." These thoughts are intruders. They can prevent you from giving your full attention to your customer and hinder you from making a sale.

Concentration and Overindulging

Believe it or not, the problem of overeating has been recognized by psychologists and medical doctors to be the result of an inability to *concentrate* on what is good and healthy for the body!

We are all experts at eating, and we keep doing it all our lives. If you want to lose weight, think about it — "think thin" as has been said. In other words, *concentrate* on losing weight. One of the best ways to do this is to make a sustained effort to give your full attention to eating and enjoying your food. That's right. If you think about your food while eating, if you let yourself savor every single bite, you will find that your body will require less, and meals will become much more pleasurable. You need to concentrate on what you are eating, how much you are eating, and where you are eating. Try it! You'll be pleasantly surprised.

Excessive smoking and drinking require concentration if they are to be managed and overcome. Smoking and drinking are generally regarded as habits. While habits are a necessary part of our ability to adapt to our environment, it is nevertheless incumbent upon us to distinguish between good habits and harmful or unnecessary habits. Smoking, drinking, and overeating do have some psychological and physiological aspects that require special attention and even professional help. Generally speaking, harmful habits can be overcome by a conscious effort to do so and by concentrating on habits that will not deprive us of good health.

Lapses in Concentration — Some Causes

We have just shown how concentration affects success and failure in a number of typical life situations. Now we will examine why we fail to concentrate. If you will give some thought to these causes, and recognize how they apply to your own problems, you will gain some valuable insights.

Stress

A person under stress can't think too clearly and certainly finds it difficult to concentrate. Yet there are some people who can concentrate and work quite well under stress. It would seem that it is not so much a matter of how much stress and worry can adversely affect concentration and thought, as how much ability one has to cope with them.

It is understandable that there are those who try to avoid dealing with serious problems. They say, "Please, I don't want to think about that now," or "I'll think about it tomorrow." However, delaying decisions, or ignoring them, does not alleviate stress and worry and does not help to solve problems. You can't really put your problems out of your mind. They will come back when you least want them.

When the mind is confronted with a tense situation, chemicals are secreted by those brain cells that serve to facilitate mental activity. If you make an effort to cope with a stressful situation, these chemicals are used in a healthy way. If you don't try to cope, but keep on procrastinating, these chemicals do not disappear. They remain in the brain and generate a condition of excitement and distraction. If anything is bothering you, it is best to deal with it immediately.

Admittedly, some problems cannot be resolved because we are powerless to deal with them. We all have had worries about things that happened in the past, or about things beyond our control. Dale Carnegie once said, "Ninety percent of the things we worry about never happen, and the other 10 percent will happen anyway." Whether Mr. Carnegie's figures are right or wrong, it's clear that many things are not worth worrying about.

Whenever you get the feeling that something is not quite right, you must make sure that your concentration in your work and other activities is not impaired. If the feeling becomes a certainty, you must determine the nature of your problem by asking yourself whether it has anything to do with your job, your family, or your emotional situation. The true nature of your problem will come to light if you do this.

While you are trying to determine the reasons for your trouble, you will be surprised to find that a number of other matters come to the surface — matters about which you were not completely aware. As you concentrate on illuminating your problems, you will be able to cope with them — and you will feel better physically and mentally.

Self-Denial — A Cause of Daydreaming

We can describe mind wandering as the phenomenon of thinking about extraneous matters when we should be concerned with those immediately at hand. Although mind wandering and daydreaming have much in common, there is an important difference: daydreaming is the phenomenon of thinking thoughts that are not entirely related to the real world.

Let us consider Ellen, a young woman with no definite aim in life. She accepted a proposal of marriage partly because all her friends were married. Years later, in the midst of an unhappy marriage, she contemplates divorce. Although she believes that she would be happier in a new life, she stops to consider the consequences. She considers the harmful emotional effects that a divorce could have on her children, but doesn't consider that they might be better off in a broken home than in an unhappy one. So she decides to stay married "for the sake of the children."

The study of the psychology of human behavior has shown that people have a way of making decisions based on certain considerations while ignoring others. Why did Ellen choose to stay in an unhappy marriage? Well, she had other considerations such as what her married friends would say if she broke up her marriage, and the gossip and rumors that would follow. It may be that these were the *real* reasons for her decision and that she rationalized when she told herself she would continue the marriage for her children's sake.

We all rationalize to some extent, but Ellen based her life on a rationalization that denied her own sincere wishes. People like Ellen are particularly prone to daydreaming and indulging in fantasies about the kind of person they would like to be or the kind of life they would like to lead. These daydreams and fantasies are symptoms of the denial of one's real self.

Psychologists say that we carry within us a mental image of the person we would like to be, and a healthy person strives to become that person. When the gap between what we imagine ourselves to be and what we really are becomes too wide, the mind will veer away from the real word and try to correct the difference by engaging in fantasies. We then develop negative feelings about ourselves; we suffer discontent and tension, and retreat into a world of fantasy and dreams.

The decisions we make have a profound bearing on our personalities. We must live with our decisions long after they are made. Too often we think only of the opinions and desires of others while ignoring our own. We would be better off if we examined and gave more weight to our own needs. This is not to say that we must never consider others or that we should become selfish and egocentric. If a certain course of action that you take benefits another, and you sincerely feel happier as a result, you have performed a fine, healthy, and self-fulfilling act. But when an action of yours which is performed for the benefit of others results in your own unhappiness and frustration, it will adversely affect your other activities. Ultimately, we should do what we regard as being right for ourselves. As Norman Vincent Peale the well-known minister said, "If you do not like yourself, who will?"

Goals and Plans

Let's look at Joe's problem once again. Does he ever concentrate for any length of time? Yes, he did once, when his boss approached him and said sternly, "You had better get this job finished by tomorrow or else ..." Joe worked at maximum effectiveness and made the deadline. Immediately after, he returned to his usual level of performance.

Joe was able to perform so well that particular time because his sense of pride in accomplishment was challenged and he was motivated to complete the job in a definite period of time. Of course, the threat of "or else ..." had something to do with his performance, but chiefly it was his wish to meet the challenge and achieve his goal.

The act of formulating goals in life enhances concentration on tasks that are directed toward those goals. You must ask yourself what you want, and work toward achieving it.

Here is a suggestion. Force yourself to describe in writing a typical day in your life as you would like it to be five years from now. This description should include the occupational status you desire and the skills, character traits, and knowledge that you will need to get along. Don't overlook putting down your ideas of what you think would give you a feeling of satisfaction and fulfillment.

Having done this, it is suggested that you write a detailed plan of the steps you must take toward the attainment of the goal or goals you have set yourself. Planning is an excellent way of organizing your thoughts and is a very efficient way of helping you to achieve what is best for you.

A Program to Become Mentally "With It"

Basically, daydreaming is an acquired habit. It may well be that we acquired this habit when we were very young. For example, if someone said no to our request for a certain toy, our mind may have wandered from the real world, and we imagined ourselves playing with the desired toy. We soon learned that such mind wandering and daydreaming brought us a measure of relaxation, and as we grew older, we acquired the habit of retreating into an unreal world that gave us much pleasure. Our minds could escape into this unreal world whenever we were faced with a task or a situation that is unpleasant or too difficult.

Well, any undesirable habit can be broken by substituting a desirable one. You can substitute the habit of paying attention for the habit of inattention. In other words, you are simply going to acquire the habit of being mentally "with it." You are going to concentrate whenever possible until the act of concentrating becomes a skill, and as with any skill, the more you use it, the better you will become.

If you are a beginner at tennis, you don't immediately hit the ball with speed and precision. Whether serving or returning, you have to start by hitting the ball easily. Gradually, as the pace increases, your game keeps improving until you are a very good tennis player.

If you are not used to paying attention, you can't suddenly acquire the habit of concentration. You must do so step by step. Start focusing your attention on easy things — things that are enjoyable and give you pleasure. The next time you are outdoors, breathe in the fresh air and really feel all the vigor and goodness that fresh air can give you. When you sit down to dinner, make sure that you give full attention to everything you eat throughout the entire meal. Think about how things taste. You don't always have to engage in aimless conversation at the table, and you don't always have to read the newspaper. Concentrated attention on your food will help you enjoy it more. Playing a game of chess or Scrabble provides good practice in concentrating, as do some card games — bridge, for example. Listening to music is a concentrating activity all by itself.

At a certain point in your attempt to develop the habit of concentration, you will have to include the art of conversation. As we noted earlier, conversing is not as easy as it seems. You have to make sure that you are giving all your attention — listening to what the other person has to say. When you are speaking, every statement you make or every question you ask should relate to the subject being discussed, and not to something irrelevant, which would indicate that your mind has been wandering.

And don't overlook the very useful activity of writing. Writing engages the kinesthetic and visual areas of the brain. When this happens, the effect on your own activities is amazing. Before going to sleep each night, record the kind of success you've had during the day in practicing concentration. You could say, "I concentrated for three songs" or "for half a meal," and the like. Be careful to think positively and express yourself in writing positive, not negative, thoughts. As you continue in this vein, you will see yourself become increasingly mentally "with it" each day. And you will experience a feeling of pride and accomplishment that will stay with you and bring you success.

Summary

This chapter sought first to show just how important the ability to concentrate is in everyday life. We saw that concentration is related to problems in numerous areas and we mentioned only a few. A few reasons for poor concentration were given, although there may be any number of emotional and physiological causes for difficulty in this area.

The key to improving concentration involves more than merely improving our abilities in distraction-prone tasks such as reading scholarly material. Concentration problems start in less noticeable ways. If your mind has been wandering all day — while walking, talking, eating, driving — it will continue to wander while reading or listening. The object is to get into the habit of concentrating.

Chapter Nine

THE ART OF RECALL

Memory suggests recall, and recall suggests memory. Are they synonymous? Not exactly, for recall is the most important manifestation of memory, and there are countless ways of recalling. Also, recall is directly related to learning, so that the better the learning, the better the recall. If you learned from and practiced the suggestions made throughout this book, it is likely that by now you will have developed considerable skill in recalling.

It is a characteristic of the way our minds work that we are more annoyed and frustrated when we cannot recall what we know than if we do not know it at all. We are angry with ourselves when things we were unable to remember yesterday come back to us with greater clarity today — when we no longer need the information. Sometimes events of long ago are recalled for no apparent reason. It is quite a feat to sort out the right memory from our extensive mental accumulations at the precise moment we want it.

Our mental activities are extremely complicated. No machine has been built — nor is it likely to be built — that can remember how to play baseball with the precision and accuracy of a human being. Though startling technological advances have made guided missiles and rockets possible (they are run by a computer which has been furnished with an electronic memory), far more miraculous is the guidance system that is involved when an outfielder goes after a fly ball. No instrument can ever come close to matching an average human being in the number of memories he has, or in his ability to process them consciously and unconsciously.

We can regard our brain as one mighty super-computer. It receives data, stores input, and recalls and processes information. A disturbance of one component may cause the entire mental process to malfunction.

Interference

It is an accepted fact that malfunction in recall occurs when extraneous matters interfere with the recall process. The businessman who tries to remember what he wants to say in a letter is bothered by the argument he had a few minutes ago. Instead of concentrating on a particular problem, you may worry about what will happen if you fail an exam: what your parents and friends will say. Then, while taking the exam, you may begin to worry that you have only ten minutes left to finish the exam. Signals in your head are warning you and saying, "Hurry, think fast." These thoughts are not helping you to recall — they are distractions.

Unconscious Factors Affecting Mental Blank

One of the most extreme forms of malfunction in recall is experiencing a mental blank during a test. Suddenly, you are unable to recall even the most elementary facts. The duration of this mental blank may last anywhere from twenty seconds to several minutes. Once the test is over, however, recall is back to normal.

It is now known that the unconscious is a major factor in causing these mental blanks. Sigmund Freud was the first to notice that much of our behavior and many of our activities are determined by the unconscious. Freud was disbelieved by many of his contemporaries. Today, however, few would deny that the unconscious exerts a powerful influence on what we remember how we remember, and how we react in certain situations.

Animal behavior is primarily nonverbal and instinctive. An animal instinctively senses danger and either retreats or tries to find some other way to protect itself. By the same token, the human being also senses and fears danger. Our instinctive reaction may be to retreat or find some other way of preserving ourselves. These instinctive reactions cannot be explained by means of logic or by trying to reach the unconscious. A person who is afflicted with a phobia may possess considerable intelligence, yet no amount of logic or persuasion will remove the phobia.

A student may not actually flee from the room where a test is being given (although unconsciously he may become ill, have a headache, or use other ploys to avoid the exam), but he will certainly experience anxiety. Anxiety may be defined as a general feeling of uneasiness. You may experience more tension than the situation you are in calls for. If the anxiety you feel is strong enough, it will interfere with recall, and the result will be a mental blank.

How to Recall

Let's suppose you want to recall the name of the ninth President of the United States. Somehow, the answer doesn't come to you, and you find yourself repeating "ninth President, ninth President" several times, hoping that the answer will come. Repeating the question often helps to evoke the answer — but there are other ways of recalling.

To remember in these instances where recall does not come easily (but where you *know* you know the answer), you must not let frustration or tension stop your mind from functioning. This chapter will show how to replace frustration with mental action.

We have discussed the fact that we can often give our memories a prod by thinking of some object or event that is related to what we want to recall. When we make a conscious effort to recall through association with an object or an event, the mind takes an alternate path.

The Spectrum of Recall

Information may be located in different areas of the brain. Memory for ideas may be located in one area, memory for words in another, and memory for one's personal thoughts in still another area.

We will mention a number of suggestions that describe ways in which you can scan the mind and retrieve information when memory fails. All involve different ways of thinking. Thinking has been called "inner communication." When you think, you send signals to your brain which reach the proper knowledge and aid in recall.

Thinking of Everything in Trying to Remember

Information is located in the brain cells and it is the task of memory to use all the possible avenues of approach to the various areas of the brain in order to draw out the desired information. If you cannot recall a person's name immediately, keep the mind moving. Think of everything relating to that person. Ask yourself if you remember the name of his spouse or sister or brother — this may very well help in retrieving the name you wish to recall. If it doesn't help, think of what the person does for a living, or of the last conversation you had together. Almost anything can serve as a trigger for recall.

Let's consider a young girl who is leaving for school in the morning and takes her umbrella along because it is raining. That evening, when she has returned home for dinner, her mother mentions a play about a man named Jacques Brel. The girl drops her spoon, jumps up, and rushes to open the door. Sure enough, the umbrella is missing and she sadly concludes that she left it somewhere.

The young girl's task now is to remember each place she had been that day, and whether or not she had the umbrella with her. This type of recall requires that she visualize putting the umbrella down and picking it up when she left a particular place. If she continues to visualize, she eventually will remember every stop she made that day, and very likely will recall where she left the umbrella. She must not give up. As long as she keeps her mind on the subject, she has a chance of strinking some memory chord that will give her the answer.

Classify Your Thoughts

A mental activity that will surely aid in recall is classifying your thoughts. If you were asked right at this moment to tell a joke, you might have trouble recalling even one. However, if you were to use a method of classification, recall would be no problem. You could search your memory for the first category — possibly a husband/wife joke. Then you would try to remember an ethnic joke, and then one about a doctor. In this way you would probably be able to recall quite a number of jokes in each category.

A student in an art history class is shown a painting and asked to name the artist. She thinks for a moment but cannot recall the correct answer. There is no reason for her to give up at that point, however. The key to unlocking the information from the depths of her mind lies in her organizing her knowledge of painters and painting. She should look at the painting and try to classify it by style or period. She may decide that it is an Impressionist painting. Then she tries to recall all the Impressionist painters she knows, and in doing this, she may come upon the name she has forgotten. If this fails, she may decide that the painting belongs to another period, and once again go down the list. Thus new avenues of transmission are opened to release knowledge.

Categorizing can be particularly effective in remembering names. If you have forgotten a name, you could think of the person's face and then ask yourself if his name starts with a *a.* Then try *b,* and so on. When you come to *j,* you may believe the name starts with that letter. Then try a few names beginning with *j,* and suddenly the name you want will be recalled. Categorizing may be a slow method of recall, but it often works when all else fails.

Draw Upon Your Own Thoughts

We have stressed the advantages of contributing your own knowledge of a subject while learning. This will keep your mind occupied, help to organize your knowledge, help in judging the value of your ideas, and increase your comprehension. We have also mentioned that we tend to remember our own thoughts better than those of others. Whenever we draw on our own thoughts in relation to a subject, an association is formed, consisting of our own ideas and opinions and any new knowledge. For example, if you remember being critical of an author or speaker, it is easy to remember why you were critical; and you will also remember particular points on which you based your criticism. Naturally, the more thoughts you had while learning, the more avenues of recall will be available to you.

Recalling your own thoughts to remember reading material can be done systematically. The surest method is to recognize your purpose in reading something. Suppose you are questioned about an article called "Victims of a Curse." Ask yourself, "What was my purpose in reading an article with such a title?" You could answer that you wanted to find out the nature of the curse, its victims and why they were cursed. This would give you a starting point for recalling your thoughts.

Reading comprehension is enhanced when you think before you start to read, particularly if it is an article about a particular subject. If you can recall how you *thought* a certain machine worked, for example, you can trigger the recall of the author's accurate description. A similar procedure can be applied to the recall of a lecture, especially if you used some of the listening suggestions discussed in the earlier chapters.

Photographic Imagery

Photographic imagery can provide you with a very good area of recall that we ordinarily don't use. We explained earlier that photographic memory involves visualizing the printed page itself rather than creating a visual experience. Although it is nearly impossible to reproduce a printed page from memory, it is possible to recall certain key sentences or terms as they appeared on the printed page.

Let's say you can visually recall the location of the term "Manifest Destiny" in the selection we talked about earlier in the book, "Life in the Antebellum Period." This can provide you with a valuable clue to finding an answer to a question that relates to "Manifest Destiny." The means by which we recall through imagery are not mysterious. With a small amount of practice, anyone can learn to recall visually.

Place-Dependent Recall

Who hasn't had the experience of being lost or unsure of the right direction while traveling? Eventually, of course, you see a landmark or some other identifying object and you know you are in the right place and are going in the right direction. This is an example of the phenomenon called place-dependent recall, which means that recall takes place best when the environment is like that in which the information was learned originally. Experiments with students have shown that those tested in the same classroom, at the same time of day, and in the same seat where the original learning took place, scored higher than a group whose testing occurred in a different place and time. And when the recall situation is different from the learning situation, the ability to recall need not be entirely lost because your mind can reconstruct the original environment. Suppose you are faced with a test question, the answer to which momentarily escapes you. If you make an effort to reproduce the environment in which your original learning took place, you will be able to visualize the printed page or your notes, and thus recall the information you need. The ability to reproduce the original learning situation is extremely effective even under conditions of severe tension because visual reproduction is less likely to be blocked.

It would be reasonable to assume from the foregoing that you can obtain the best results by studying in the same place and at the same time of day. Carrying this a bit further, it would also seem logical to study each subject in a different setting, providing you are consistent.

When All Attempts Fail

If after you have reorganized your knowledge, drawn your conclusions, used photographic imagery, re-created the original learning environment, and thought of everything that is related to a subject, and you still cannot recall, there is one last resource if you have enough time. Simply pack your problem into your unconscious mind and wait. If you can eliminate your nervousness and irritability, you will be able to recall without too much effort. You can facilitate this process by vocalizing your intention to remember. You may say, "I know that I know Betty's birthday. I want to recall it. I will recall it." Say it aloud, clearly and earnestly. Then relax and think of something else — your brain will surely respond to the sound of your voice and help you to recall.

Exercises in Recall

Here are some exercises to get the various parts of your brain communicating:

1. At the end of a day, try to recall everything you did that day by visualizing each activity. One activity will serve to recall another. Your final recall should be a chronological recap of the day.

2. The following game can be a lot of fun. It requires the same kind of mental activity as recall. List the letters of the alphabet in order, one under the other. Then have someone call out a sentence. Some famous statement will do. Across from each letter of the alphabet write the corresponding letters of the sentence, as illustrated below.

A	D	J	R	S	L
B	A	K	P	T	L
C	M	L	E	U	S
D	N	M	D	V	P
E	T	N	O	W	E
F	H	O	E	X	E
G	E	P	S	Y	D
H	T	Q	F	Z	A
I	O	R	U		

Treat the resulting pairs of letters as the initals of famous people. Your objective is to be able to supply the names of these famous people. For the first set of initials, you may say "Alvin Dark," for the former baseball manager. This game should be played competitively and it should be timed. That will stimulate pressure. You may decide that the person or couple who can think of the most names in a given period, say 10 minutes, wins. The technique here is to keep the mind active. Keep trying names to yourself. Never let the mind go blank. You should also categorize information. Think first of people in sports, then entertainment, politics, and so on. This game is exciting, challenging, good practice, and fun.

3. This is the well-known "concentration game." An ordinary deck of playing cards is spread face down on a table. Two or three players each overturn two cards. The player who overturns the two matching cards (matching in number not in suit) gets to put that pair in his pile. The player who has the largest pile at the end wins. The key factor here is to remember the location of the cards that were overturned. Because children naturally visualize, even five-year-olds can compete with adults in this game.

Summary

As we have seen, to recall most effectively is to apply all the resources at your disposal. Many things are only temporarily forgotten and you should not give up on them until you have examined all related memories and associations. This means that you must reconstruct each learning situation, recall your own thoughts on a subject, utilize photographic imagery, and remember your own actions. In this way anything can start a chain of memories rolling back.

Chapter Ten

THE PHYSIOLOGY OF MEMORY

Simply reading this chapter won't help you to improve your ability to remember or concentrate any more than reading a manual on the mechanics of an automobile will teach you how to drive it. Nevertheless, if you have fully absorbed the ideas and principles discussed in the preceding chapters, and if you are applying them toward the improvement of your memory, your mind will be receptive to what follows. No one can ever be truly knowledgeable about a subject unless he or she has some idea of *why* certain methods and procedures work. When you see the reason behind a certain action, that action is performed better. This chapter will give you an insight into the human mind and its workings.

The function of memory is essentially threefold: the brain must receive information; it must store and retain that information, and it must allow access to that information when it is needed.

How Data Is Transmitted

Data is transmitted through the environment by light rays, sound waves, and by our sense of touch. The brain cannot deal with all the different types of "input" in their original form; they must be converted into a form that the nervous system can accept.

The actual process by which the brain, in conjunction with the senses, converts the rays and waves received from the environment are not within the scope of this book. Suffice it to say that all data transmitted by the nervous system is converted into a form of electrical impulse. Electrical impulses are transmitted to various parts of the nervous system and the brain by means of a special cell called a *neuron*. (See fig. 1.) The electrical impulses transmitted to the neurons are representative of the input rays and waves. If the sound waves, for example, are received by the ear at a certain rate, the neuron will react at the same rate, in a sequence of on-and-off spurts. In this manner the signal is preserved. Actually, the process is considerably more complicated. Numerous neurons, sometimes thousands, participate in the transmission of a single input signal.

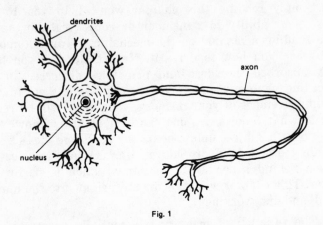

Fig. 1

You will notice in figure 1 that a neuron is comprised of three main parts: the dendrites, the axon, and the cell body which contains the nucleus. The end of the axon branches off into a number of terminal twigs. Nerve impulses travel in only one direction. Sensations are first felt by the dendrites and the signal is passed through the cell body to the axon.

Neurons transmit their electrical impulses to other neurons across a very narrow juncture called a *synapse*. The human brain contains an estimated 10 to 15 billion neurons. Each has its dendrites, axons, and terminal twigs, hence an incalculable number of synapses.

Transmission of the signal across the synapse is a chemical process that occurs in all directions in spurts or waves. The wave pattern corresponds to the pattern of activating the neuron. In other words, the representation of the original signal is still retained and transmitted.

Where Memory Is Located

It is generally believed that the nervous system is capable of transmitting memories to cells within the brain, where they can be stored in some way. Many scientists believe that everything experienced or learned produces some physical change in the brain. Where do these signals go? Where are they stored when they are not present in the consciousness?

The cerebral cortex, the outer layer of the brain, is the structure generally believed to be concerned with thought, learning, and memory and with the recognition of objects and symbols. Studies have shown that in animals further along in the evolutionary process the cerebral cortex is larger and has more convolutions (folds) relative to the rest of the nervous system. The mouse has a more highly developed cortex than most fish. The cortex of the monkey is more developed than the mouse. And the cortex of man more developed than that of the monkey. The size and weight of the brain is not the key factor. The cat does not have a larger cortex than the alligator, yet the relative size of the cat's cortex compared with the rest of its body indicates that the cat is the more intelligent animal.

It has been shown that the cortex can enlarge and develop, depending on the activities and the environment of an organism. In one study young rats were divided into two groups. The first group was raised in a stimulating environment and was taught a number of tricks. The second group was raised in an impoverished environment lacking stimulation. After a period of several months, the stimulated rats demonstrated superior learning ability. Later examination revealed a sizeable difference in the weight of the cortex of these rats.

Thus it appears that the cortex is the area most involved in learning, retention, and recall. Continued experimentation concentrated on determining a more exact location of function. Stimulation of a certain area in conscious patients undergoing brain surgery created vivid, complex memories. A girl who had a portion of her skull exposed during the course of an operation said that when a certain area was touched by a needle, she heard familiar music so clearly that she believed a phonograph had been turned on. Stimulation of all other areas did not reveal these experiences. Memory for language appears to lie in the dominant hemisphere of the cortex (i.e. the left side for right-handed people). Damage to this area leads to a condition known as *aphasia,* which is characterized by an inability to understand the written or spoken word.

Despite this seemingly convincing evidence supporting localization, it appears that valid objections can be raised against it, the most forceful of which is that if a certain brain tissue known to be essential in memory of a response is cut, the result will be that although the animal forgets the response, it will take fewer trials for relearning, thus indicating that "saving" has taken place. Saving occurs when after having once learned something, which is later forgotten, we find that we can relearn it in a shorter time than originally. This suggests that some memory existed elsewhere and that some other area was able to assume its functions. It seems reasonable to conclude that data is routed through the nerve tracts to certain places on the cortex where similar knowledge and experiences are stored. However, traces of these experiences are also routed to more than one cell and to different locations. Memories of visual experiences are routed to certain areas, memories of hearing, touch, and smell to still others. Thus storage for a single experience may be located in a number of cells at various positions on the cortex.

Any experience is comprised of a number of visual, verbal, and tactile, or kinesthetic, memories. Throughout the brain, there are innumerable interconnections and passageways that serve to tie these memories together so that the recall of one memory can trigger the recall of an entire experience. Events can be recalled by hearing a sound, seeing a place again, or feeling something familiar. By hearing, seeing, or feeling only one small portion of an event, the entire event can be recalled through the use of these interconnections.

It holds true then that the more areas of the brain that can be utilized to store an experience, the more easily will an experience be recalled. This hypothesis is behind our suggestions to store knowledge, using as many mental faculties as possible. Later in recall, if only one area can be tapped, it will start a chain reaction bringing forth memories from other areas of the brain. By using as many areas as possible, we will have alternative paths for recall should the primary path be blocked.

We discussed long- and short-term memory earlier in the book. It is believed that short-term memory involves a closed circuit of neurons where electronic signals reverberate (circulate) after the signals are received from the sensory neurons. In the meantime, the signal strives to cross the synapse to other neurons that are connected to cells of long-term memory.

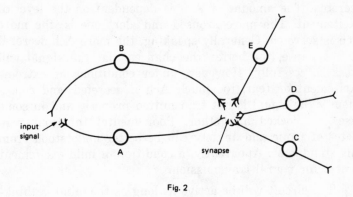

Fig. 2

Referring to figure 2, let us examine what is probably a greatly simplified illustration of the theory of consolidation. An electronic signal is transmitted along neuron *A* to the synapse, where it is transmitted to neuron *B*. The two form a reverberating circuit.

Neurons *C, D,* and *E* at the synaptic juncture also have the potential to receive the signal. However, it is extremely important for an understanding of this subject to know that *transmission of a signal across the synapse does not always occur.* If this were not the case, if the signal were to be picked up by all the neurons at a synapse, messages would be sprayed indiscriminately to all parts of the brain. There would be no means whereby messages could be routed and controlled. There would be no means of discriminating, sorting, and selecting important data. On the other hand, if the signal does successfully cross the synapse, learning will occur, and consolidation will take place.

What Determines Receptivity

Whether the signal will be received by neuron D for example, and be transmitted to long-term areas, depends upon the state of the synapse, the length of time that the signal is kept reverberating, and the receptivity of neuron D to that particular signal. The state of the synapse depends on the amount of chemicals (Acetylcholine, or Ach) secreted. The amount of Ach is dependent on the level of excitement. The more aroused and alert one is, the more Ach is secreted. Generally speaking, the more Ach secreted at a synapse, the better the chances that the signal will cross successfully. However, under conditions of extreme excitement or fear, too much Ach is secreted, and consequently the signal is not transmitted properly and in some cases is blocked altogether. Poor mental functioning in states of panic and anxiety can be better understood from this standpoint. Apparently, a condition of mild excitement is best for neural transmission.

The circuit will be active as long as the mind is thinking about a particular experience or thought. The longer the signal is kept in short-term memory, the more cells will be affected by the signal. The signal will have more time to cross the synapse and be transmitted to longer term areas. That is why repetition aids retention.

The key question at this point involves the notion of receptivity. What makes a neural cell receptive to a signal? Why do some neurons receive certain signals and reject other signals?

In a sense, the memory signal may be thought of as looking for a place in which to settle. If the input signal has a special meaning for the person, if there is a relationship between what is being learned and something that has been learned previously, the reverberating signal will find its way to the cells harboring the prior knowledge.

The more relationships a thought has, the more likely that its signals will find a place to lodge. Science is quite hazy on the neurobiological actions underlying the reasons for this selective receptivity. However, laboratory studies have observed electrical waves passing over the cerebral cortex during learning. Furthermore, these waves differ in kind with different types of learning. It also has been observed that all cells in the cortex are in a constant state of firing, though their voltage levels are relatively low. The cells discharge in the form of electrical pulses and these cells take on a distinctive pattern of discharge. We may then conjecture that the signal will be received by cells or a group of cells that have similar patterns. The neurons that connect these cells with synapses in the short-term area must have some way of feeling and sensing this pattern and tend to attract signals in short-term memory that have similar frequencies.

Perhaps this concept can be better understood if we see a similarity here with the reception of radio and television signals. These signals are carried through the air at a certain frequency and will only be transmitted to, and received by, the antennas of those sets that are "tuned in" to the correct frequency or channel. Thus, when a radio set is tuned to 500 kilocycles, it will only receive signals at that frequency. All others will be rejected. The antenna may be thought of as being analogous to the connecting neuron, and the radio as being analogous to a group of cells in the long-term area of the brain.

Remember that there are a multitude of neurons meeting at a synapse. Signals have a number of possible alternatives. Each synapse has its minute electrochemical decisions to make. Due to the complex interconnections of axons and dendrites, eight hundred or more neurons may meet at a synaptic juncture. The impulse may or may not cross the synapse. If it does, it will be picked up by one or more neurons. Some of these neurons may connect to unrelated memories and may then trigger a series of recollections that are unrelated to whatever a person may be reading about. However, when consciously awakened, the cells containing the chemistry of the old knowledge are activated. The cells are then more receptive and attract the incoming signal by making the path of connecting neurons more excitable. That is why the emphasis on such concepts as reading for a purpose, thinking, and hypothesizing before actually starting to read are so important.

Of course, this discussion on consolidation has been greatly simplified. There may actually be hundreds or even thousands of synapses or circuits operating in short-term memory and the connecting neurons take far more complex paths than just indicated, but the basic principles appear sound.

What Memory Is Made Of

When we recall knowledge and use it for a period of time, we have taken something from our subconscious mind and brought it to consciousness. What form has this knowledge actually taken between the time it was learned and the moment we use it? Furthermore, we cannot help but marvel at the cohesiveness of our stored memories. It is not necessary to recall all events in chronological order should we wish to remember a specific event. We recall events that are seemingly undisturbed by other experiences and when we wish to recall something we can do so without being bombarded by an avalanche of other memories. (While it is true that other branches of psychology particularly the study of perception, will show that memories, especially those containing an emotional significanse, are altered by the dynamics of the personality, the basic experience nevertheless remains cohesive.)

We must now inquire as to the nature of this wondrous storage mechanism. What constitutes storage after the signals reach the cells? Do the cells retain the original representation of the idea by continuing electrical activity? Or are the chemical and physical nature of the cells storing the memories reconstructed in some way? Recent developments have made most psychologists support the view that a change takes place in the chemistry of the cells. The various chemical changes are representative of memories when they are in a subconscious or resting state.

The neurons in the brain are surrounded by other cells which do not conduct electrically. They are called neuroglia, or glia. The glia as well as neurons contain a chemical called RNA (ribonucleic acid). RNA is similar to DNA (deoxyribonucleic acid), which has been established as the substance within the genes that determines hereditary characteristics. In DNA the genes carry a memory for growth and development.

There is a multitude of somewhat incredulous evidence implicating RNA as the possible memory molecule. It is found in the nuclei of neural and glia cells. It's concentration decreases in old age, much as memorizing ability does, and it has been reported that RNA supplements in diets of aged persons improve their memory.

Perhaps the most dramatic experiment on this subject was performed on albino rats. Two groups of rats learned to approach a food cup and obtain a food pellet when a stimulus was presented. The stimulus for one group was a flashing light, the other group responded to a clicking sound. The rats were then killed. RNA was extracted from them and then injected into those rats that had never been exposed to either situation. Six of the eight "click injected" rats then responded to the click, and seven of the eight "light injected" rats responded only to the light. Many other experiments of this type have been conducted with similar results.

RNA is a very long, slender molecule containing four base chemicals. These bases may appear in any sequence. The sequential order appears to be a code containing representations of experiences. Young rats were trained to walk a tightrope to reach food on a platform. After they had learned to perform the feat well, they were killed along with other rats that had not been trained. The nerve cells associated with recognition of balance cues were then examined. The results showed significant differences in the sequential order of the bases between the experimental and control groups, while the RNA of the experimental group all had distinct sequential similarities. Therefore, if one molecule is about 4,000 links long, that means that the number of different combinations of the molecule would be 4^{2000}. Multiply this number by the billions of neural and glia cells in the brain and you can get an idea of the fantastic amount of information that the brain has the capacity to store. Of course, we do not know the code as yet or just what constitutes a unit of information.

The RNA theory had one drawback to its acceptance. It had been shown that the level of RNA of a cell involved in learning builds up to a peak shortly after the learning experience, but then gradually subsides, so that it is back to a normal level after about twenty-four hours. Since memories can exist for far longer than twenty-four hours, it was doubted that RNA was the actual memory molecule.

It now appears that the function of RNA is to direct the assembly of the protein structure in the cells. RNA permanently alters the structure of the cells, but the memory is retained over a long period by the protein formation of the cells.

A brilliant experiment on this subject was conducted by George Ungar and Wolfgang Parr, the eminent psychologists. Rats, who normally like the dark, were given a shock every time they approached darkness. Eventually, as a consequence, they had been taught to fear the dark. Then a substance derived from their brain tissue was injected into rats and white mice that had not been taught this fear. Afterward, the injected rats and mice also avoided darkness.

After experimenting further and chemically analyzing the brain extracts, it was believed that a particular sequence of amino acids (a protein is comprised of amino acids) was responsible for the association of darkness and shock. To check this hypothesis, the substance was duplicated, not from brain extracts, but rather from laboratory chemicals. Once again, the injected animals showed fear of the dark. Thus, for the first time, man has gained some insight into the chemical code in which memory is stored.

The code itself consists of more than just the original input representation. It is far more complicated than that. By the time a signal reaches long-term storage, it becomes integrated with signals from other cells in the brain and the result is a mixture. When two or more cells combine signals, a new chemical structure is created, and that is the physical basis of learning and the formation of associations. An association is probably formed when two bits of information are located in the same cell.

Conclusion

It has been said that the more one learns, the more one becomes conscious of one's own ignorance. This is certainly true in the study of memory. We still have very little idea of the method that cells use to transform electrical impulses into chemical codes; only that it appears to be done and that RNA and the protein structures of cells are involved.

Then there is the process of recall. We can assume that the mechanisms involved are the same in that it is basically accomplished by neurons, synapses, and cellular chemicals, but we do not know how this reverse process works. We can only assume that there is some means by which the stored chemical knowledge is tapped and that it reverts back to electrical impulses, and finally to the actual images and verbal reproductions that comprise our conscious thought. It is possible that conscious thought involves a duplication of a short- and long-term memory system but in reverse. If we accept the localization theory, then memories are located in various parts of the brain. The short-term circuit in recall then would serve to hold signals that attract similar signals from the diverse areas of the cortex. There they are integrated into thought.

More is being learned each day and a greater knowledge of the recall process appears certain in the near future. We have come a long way from the days when the concept of mind involved an explanation in supernatural terms. We know that the mind is capable of storing voluminous information in our waking state and that it sorts out portions of this information for long-term storage. Most important of all, we now know enough to use some concepts from physiology and relate them to memory improvement. Improving memory consists first of those techniques that will facilitate the process of consolidation, and second, those techniques that will help our minds locate the knowledge when we wish to retrieve it. A good way to review the principles in this book is to imagine how each in turn will aid memory from a physiological standpoint.

Of course, the physiological description of the neural and chemical basis of memory has been greatly simplified for our purposes. The actual process is probably of sufficient complexity to stagger imagination. Certainly more than two neurons make up the short-term circuit. They form synaptic connections with perhaps millions of neurons, and perhaps memories are lodged in countless cells combining to form a past experience. In addition, over a thousand different types of chemicals have been identified as operating in our brains; the functions of many of them are unknown.

Summary

It is now possible to return to the basic question of how learning experiences are received, stored, and then recalled.

Data from the environment is in the form of waves and variations in pressure. Our senses respond to the pattern of variations and transmit the pattern to the nervous system, where it is converted to electronic impulses. These impulses are representative of the original pattern of wave and pressure variations. The impulses are carried along cell bodies, called neurons, which meet at synaptic connections. Chemical conditions as well as the receptivity of the connecting neurons determine whether the signal will cross the synapses and learning will occur.

Storage of learning signals appears to be located in the chemical formation of protein structures in neural and glia cells on the cerebral cortex. Indications are that RNA found in the nuclei of neurons, is involved in the transition process necessary in converting electrical impulses into chemical form.

Our knowledge is still scanty as to just how recall occurs. The belief is that in its underlying principles knowledge is retrieved chemically, is converted into electrical impulses, and is then manifested as conscious memory.

Chapter Eleven

HOW YOU CAN GET OTHERS TO REMEMBER
WHAT YOU HAVE SAID AND DONE

Exasperating as our own memory failure can some-times be, what is even more exasperating to us is when others do not remember what we said, what instructions we gave or requests we made, or what tasks we assigned.

At today's fast-moving pace, communication, whether it relates to the expression of thoughts or ideas in speech or writing, or in the performance of tasks, is of the great-est importance. For successful communication, two ele-ments must be present: the information must be communi-cated or expressed or presented by the sender, and the receiver must accept and retain it. This chapter will show you how you can use the principles of memory to com-municate successfully; that is, how you can assure reten-tion so that successful communication takes place.

Some time ago my wife and I were greatly concerned because our two-year-old son loved to run out into the street outside our home. The street is heavily trafficked, and although we were aware of the danger, we hesitated to resort to harsh measures to restrain him. It doubtless did not take the boy long to learn that he should not play in the street, but like so many of us, he would forget when seized with the irresistible temptation to do what he knew he should not do.

One Saturday night, when my wife and I were going out to dinner, our baby-sitter brought with her a copy of *Mad Magazine*. The back cover had a cartoon of a man walking across a street and being hit by a car. The pe-destrian signal spelled *SUE* instead of *WALK* or *DONT WALK*. The picture of the man as he was hit by the car was grossly exaggerated and absurdly contorted.

Right then and there a plan for successful communication occurred to me. The very next day I told my son that I was going to tell him a story. In telling the story, I greatly exaggerated the details, pointing out the parts of the body that were "messed up" by the "terrible crash." I then asked him to think about what it would be like if a car hit *him*.

Awful you say? A child shouldn't be exposed to such terrifying details at such a young age? Well, the fact is that from then on he would not go out into the street for the largest candy bar in the world. I could almost see him remembering the terrifying details every time he looked out into the street.

Why was I able to get through to him? I was able to reach him because the idea of being hit by a car and the possible pain was an emotional experience for him. Furthermore, I didn't just tell him what could happen, I *showed* him. He was able to conjure a visual image of the event and remember it with all its accompanying emotion.

Can the principles just discussed be used to communicate information to adults as well? Of course they can, along with all the other principles discussed in Chapter 2. Let's examine four areas in which these principles can be applied while you add some ideas from your own experience and knowledge.

The Teacher

The teacher or instructor is in a most favorable position for utilizing the principles of memory. He (or she) can fix a lesson in the minds of students by using visual aids and auxiliary materials. These, more than words, can sometimes help to strengthen concentration and memory. If, for example, the lesson is about how a certain machine works, the instructor can begin by showing pictures of the machine and indicating the purpose for which it was devised; then, the basic principles upon which the machine operates can be explained. Whatever the subject, properly organized information supported by such teaching aids as can be visualized and translated into pertinent associations are prime aids to retention.

The Salesman

A salesman facing a possible buyer needs the direct, person-to-person approach. No matter what the item — an insurance plan, a cosmetic, a vacuum cleaner — the salesman must *communicate* so that the prospective buyer will remember what the salesman said, the salesman himself, and the product offered.

I started out by selling Rapid Reading courses to schools. The usual procedure was to see the principal first. On one occasion, I had to see the assistant principal because the principal was handling an emergency. This was my situation: I had to present my program to the assistant principal, who would present it (favorably, I hoped) to the principal, who would present it to the superintendent, who would present it to the Board of Education.

Quite a chain of communication! It's axiomatic that whenever information is communicated verbally, it decreases quantitatively and qualitatively. Had I been more experienced and wiser, I would not have wasted my time presenting my materials to the assistant principal. I would have made an excuse for coming some other time. I went through the presentation quite well, and the assistant principal said it all sounded very good and he would speak to the principal about it. I left, satisfied, but I didn't know that I didn't have a ghost of a chance of making the sale.

If you are a salesman you must remember that the middleman is not personally motivated to present information to his superior — that is not what he is paid for. Yet, if there is only one middleman to deal with, selling to him can be managed successfully by helping his retention and recall through questions.

For example, I could have divided my product, a reading course, into three categories. I could have first asked if the program I was proposing would benefit his employees. If the answer is yes, I would ask how he feels about our company's references. Finally, I would ask his opinion of our price.

As to the middleman, in answering my questions, he is unconsciously organizing my presentation into three major areas that will certainly help him to retain the information. He will recall the references, how my price compares with others, and so on. Mostly, however, he will be favorably disposed to the presentation I made, and at the same time he will remember his own words.

Don't hesitate to ask questions. Let's look at the matter this way. As a result of my presentation, he should be sold personally. The problem is to make sure that he remembers and conveys what he remembers when he has to speak to others. If the middleman is not personally sold at this point — if his answers to my questions have been negative — the sale can't be made. On the other hand, if his answer to one of the questions was indefinite, then all the questions have been of value, because I now know what area or areas should be strengthened with greater sales emphasis.

A top salesman I know uses another excellent technique. At the beginning of his presentation he says, "Now, you know your business better than I, so I'm not going to tell you how this computer system will help. What I'll do is simply go over the benefits of our system, and perhaps you can see where our system may be more helpful to you. This is a challenge to the man because he will be in a position to remember his own thoughts about the presentation.

Visual sales material is certainly helpful. If the sales material is in the form of a brochure or other printed matter, allow the customer time to examine it — it will enhance concentration. Letting the customer turn the pages will also bring his own physical movements into play and that enhances retention. If you are a car salesman it is imperative that the prospective customer at least get into the car if not actually drive it. Later, when he is more serious about buying, the remembered experience will be a subconscious motivating force.

The Public Speaker

Research has indicated that less than 25 percent of any lecture or speech is remembered. I once thought this an incredible statistic, and yet, it is very likely correct.

In a lecture or speech before a large audience, personal contact and involvement are absent. As a result, the speaker must see to it that his speech is concise and clear, and that all the important points are presented and summarized.

A speaker can help an audience prepare to receive information by stating his objectives at the very beginning. Any divergence from the stated objective or theme can cause interference and result in even less retention. Statements like, "That reminds me of the time when ..." had better relate well to the main theme or the anecdotes may be remembered and the speech forgotten.

The earlier reference to emotional involvement as an aid to memory and retention concerned an incident with a child, but this device works equally well with adults. People will remember a feeling much more strongly than they will a word or a statistic. We have all been part of an audience that has listened to a speaker who, though perhaps poorly organized and getting nowhere, was nevertheless so emotional that he carried us along on his own tide of feeling.

One of the best techniques for getting an audience involved emotionally is to replace statistics with personal experiences or with a story. The story of a single family's ordeal following a flood will do more for memory than columns of statistics about property damage caused by the flood. People identify with people, not with numbers.

Interpersonal Communication

Roy Garn in his book *The Power of Emotional Appeal* made this interesting — and true — statement: "All speaking is public speaking." Every suggestion in the preceding section holds true whether you are speaking in public or to an individual. A single listener is just as affected by the principles of organization as is a large audience. The more quickly you, the speaker, come to the point, the more your listener or listeners will absorb and recall.

A person-to-person situation is likely to generate greater variation in emotional response than a large audience situation. Reaching a person's emotions aids retention, of course, but it is important to note that people react differently and that their emotional responses vary greatly in any given circumstance. The variations are caused by the unique psychological makeup of each person. Mr. Garn also said that each person responds to a certain stimulus — each has a certain emotional soft spot. When you know that soft spot — whether it is money, romance, curiosity, self-presentation, or recognition — you can communicate more effectively.

Summary

Learn to communicate better and your audience will remember better. I once told a secretary that a number to be called was 3342. Noting the rather hectic circumstances in the office, and knowing the young lady, I decided to go a bit further. "Did you know that 3342 B.C. is the year the Sphinx was built in Egypt?" I asked. "How interesting," she said with a sigh. Well, maybe it wasn't interesting or true, but she remembered the number. If you don't want people to forget your birthday, you can use the same idea of adding a little *thought* when you mention the date, such as, "I was born two days before Christmas," or "I was born three days after the beginning of spring."

Chapter Twelve

MEMORY AND SUCCESS

Your ultimate goal in studying memory is self-improvement. As you no doubt know, the human organism is extremely complex. Memory is intricately interwoven with other psychological functions, including the drive for self-improvement and the development of personality. With this in mind, we will now take an inward look that is beyond the world of books.

There are a great many individual differences in the ability to learn and perform acts that involve muscular control. These differences occur even within the same person. Someone may learn and improve in tennis at a remarkable rate, be only fair at learning to type, and be completely hopeless on the dance floor, no matter how much instruction is received.

Practice and repetition refine the pathways which lead from the muscles being used to that part of the brain that houses the memory for the performance of skill. It would be reasonable to assume that to the muscles and nerves, the type of activity would make no difference — that learning one skill would be no more difficult and no easier than learning another. But there *is* a difference — and we can assume that it is psychological.

Perception

Have you ever noticed how two people can give completely different versions of the same occurence? Have you ever noticed how slowly time passes when you are anxiously awaiting someone? These two examples involve the mental quality of perception. *How* something appears to you depends on your particular psychological makeup — a makeup that allows you to perceive what you look at or experience in your own way, no matter how distorted or imaginary it may be.

Your Own Beliefs About Yourself

It is entirely normal — and healthy — for you to perceive the world around you in accordance with your own emotions, memories, beliefs, experiences, and the way in which you perceive yourself. You may remember that when you were ten years old, a person of twenty-five seemed old. At a later time of your life, twenty-five didn't seem old at all — prime examples of how personal beliefs influence perception.

Situations, tasks, goals, and objectives also depend on your beliefs about yourself. You might, for instance, perceive tennis, dancing, typing, or taking a test as difficult. At this point we realize that, faced with the problem of difficulty, a person may be said to be lacking in confidence. A low level of confidence will cause a correspondingly poor use of your abilities, while a high level of confidence will enable you to make full use of your abilities.

Self-Concepts and Memory

Beliefs about yourself are largely formed by memories of past experiences. Memories of success or failure may cause you to declare, "I am a good athlete," or "I am a poor dancer" — and they may well affect your confidence in a multitude of areas. How these memories are constructed, or the form they take, depends first on the actual experiences you have had, and second — and far more important — on how these experiences are remembered.

One student may receive a grade of 80 on a test and remember it as a success. Another may receive the same grade and remember it as just the opposite. The crucial factor is, what will you do with these memories? Will you use them to strengthen your abilities in the direction of success, or will you allow yourself to constantly dwell on your failures and thus lessen your chances of success? Thomas Edison suffered many failures througout his entire life, but his memories of these only served to spur him on to greater and greater successes.

How You Can Affect Your Memory System

A startling experiment has shown how memory can affect performance. Two groups of students of equal scholastic ability were asked to write a composition. One group was to describe the saddest event in their lives; the other group was to describe the happiest even in their lives, then they all took the same math test. When all the scores were tabulated, those that had remembered the happy event scored significantly higher on the math test. This would seem to indicate that establishing the habit of remembering success tends to promote success.

Keep a written record of your successful experiences — especially those that gave you a feeling of pride and satisfaction — any experience, from how you learned to ride a bicycle to the congratulations you received for helping someone with the dishes. The act of writing will make these memories of pride and satisfaction part of you and your thoughts for the future. Then whenever a tense or threatening situation approaches, such as a test, interview, etc., recall your successful moments.

Creating Memories for a Specific Situation

Whether or not you have had successful experiences in a specific situation does not matter. We can program our minds to act as spontaneously as we would like to act by creating experiences. Look at it this way. We often say to ourselves that we would like to act more this way or that in a given situation. Then the moment arrives and we become so involved in the predicament that we forget how we wanted to behave. To some degree it is a problem of memory. We can program our minds to act in a certain way in much the same manner as we do to remember other things. We can and should create the anticipated situation as clearly as possible, add any problems, and then on our own cinemascope screen, we can see ourselves behaving exactly as we would like to see ourselves in that situation.

This situation will be just as potent a factor as any other memory, perhaps more so, because we shall consciously review our created images over and over again.

The mind strives for consistency. Put happy, successful thoughts in our minds and we will spontaneously tend to act in accordance with our thoughts.

If we spend our time while waiting for an employment interview thinking about all the things that we can say or do wrong, we are implanting negative thoughts in our minds and adversely affecting our future actions.

AFTERWORD

It is my hope that all the principles, methods, and techniques discussed in this book will be of practical value to you in your everyday life. In the first two chapters, in which I gave the reasons for forgetting and the basic principles involved, I endeavored to show the *why* and the *how* behind these principles.

Yet, for this book to achieve its ultimate value to you, more than knowing the why and how of improving your memory and concentration is needed. The knowledge and skills you have acquired should be extended and developed through constant application. If, in addition to strengthening your memory and your ability to concentrate, this book has helped you to become more aware of how your mind works, then it has achieved its highest purpose.

Acknowledgments

The Metropolitan Museum of Art

Alexander, John White. *Walt Whitman* (1889). Oil on canvas, 50" x 40". The Metropolitan Museum of Art, New York. Gift of Mrs. Jeremiah Milbank, 1961. Used with permission.

Goya y Lucientes, Francesco de. *Pepito Costa y Bonells*. Oil on canvas, 41 3/8" x 33 1/4". The Metropolitan Museum of Art, New York. Gift of Countess Bismarck, 1961. Used with permission.

Mobil Oil Corporation

for the excerpt "What went wrong?" from the pamphlet *Toward a National Energy Policy*, Mobil Oil Corporation. Reprinted by permission.

The Museum of Modern Art

Cézanne, Paul. *Still Life with Apples* (1895–98). Oil on canvas, 27" x 36 1/2". The Museum of Modern Art, New York. Lillie P. Bliss Collection. Used with permission.

Degas, Hilaire-Germain-Edgar. *At the Milliner's* (c. 1882). Pastel, 27 5/8" x 27 3/4". The Museum of Modern Art, New York. Gift of Mrs. David M. Levy. Used with permission.

Hopper, Edward. *Gas* (1940). Oil on canvas, 26 1/4" x 40¼". The Museum of Modern Art, New York. Mrs. Simon Guggenheim Fund. Used with permission.

NASA Facts

for the excerpt "Venus Observed," NASA Facts, 1968 (NF-13-4-63).

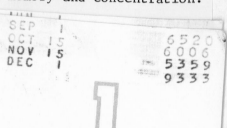